# FINDING HOPE IN THE DARKNESS

## Jonathan Yandell

FWB
Publications
The Best is Less

**FWB**
**FWB Publications**
Columbus, Ohio

# ENDORSEMENTS

We read Jonathan Yandell's story with great emotion and empathy -- not just because our families are close and our struggles are similar – but because this is a great book, well-written, honest, revealing, uplifting. Jonathan takes us on a tour of his life with Multiple Sclerosis and leaves us with a testimony of God's all-sufficient grace.

--Robert and Katrina Morgan
Author & Teaching Pastor at The Donelson Fellowship

Jonathan reveals the ugliness of MS while highlighting the determination and grace in which he navigated life. By far, Jonathan has given us more than the disease has taken from him. He has taught me a lot as a colleague and now as an author. Through these pages, you will get vicarious peeks into some "behind the scenes" rawness, not for pity but to reveal handiwork of God on imperfect lives. While reading about Jonathan, this story will encourage you in life's obstacles and give you a glimpse at God's perspective.

--Ron Hunter Jr., Ph.D.
Executive Director & CEO of Randall House

While MS is an ugly and complicated disease, what my good friend Jonathan has written is beautiful and easy to read. I have always loved to hear Jonathan speak--because he grabs and maintains your attention with his original insights and authenticity. Reading his book is no different. I couldn't put it down until I finished it. It will challenge and encourage you.

--Susan Turnbough
*Senior Trainer*
International Training Alliance

"I cannot remember reading a book that has moved me more than Jonathan Yandell's book in which he gives insight into the daily life of one suffering from a debilitating illness like MS. I must say, it was riveting. It held my attention from beginning to end. I cried some, laughed some, almost shouted in a few places. This book is a must read, not only for those facing the harsh realities of a long-term illness, but for those of us who have no idea about the struggle many of our friends face just to make it through another day. The book is inspiring, encouraging, and challenging. This is a story that needed to be told."

--Glenn Poston, Promotional Director
Tennessee State Association of Free Will Baptists

This book is dedicated
to my wife, Dianna Yandell.
Thanks for showing me every day
that no one loves me more
than you and Jesus.

# PREFACE

I was a fifth grader, a member of Mrs. Carmichael's class at John Sutter Elementary in Modesto, California when a guest speaker came to class. A congenial young man, he related well to the students. I don't remember his name or even his face, but I remember his occupation (he was an author) . . . and his wheelchair.

If the cause of his disability was specified, I don't remember it. But, I do remember thinking how great it was that he was able to write in spite of his handicap. I cannot recall the exact nature of his writing (articles, books, etc.), but I clearly remember the impression he made on me.

As I walked several blocks home after school, I thought, *I should pay attention in school and learn how to write well so that I will still have a way to make a living if I ever end up in a wheelchair.*

When I shared the story with one of my caregivers, she immediately concluded "That was prophetic!" I don't know if she is right, but it is at least curious that I have written a book after being forced to face life from a chair of my own due to multiple sclerosis.

Prophetic or not, I never imagined writing a volume like the one you hold in your hands, a chronicle of my life with MS and the lessons I have learned along the way. It is an intensely personal account, pulling back the curtain on portions of the journey I never thought I would share.

I have done this with the full knowledge that this could be misinterpreted, but I've done so with the clear conviction that this transparency was essential. My deepest desire is not you would admire me or bemoan my fate (indeed, others have suffered much more with greater composure), but rather that you would applaud our glorious God for his sustaining grace.

It is my prayer that you find hope in these pages. The apostle Paul said it well: "May the God of hope fill you with all joy and peace as you trust in him, so that you may overflow with hope by the power of the Holy Spirit" (Romans 15:13).

Jonathan

# Table of Contents

# Darkness Grows

# Introduction to Part 1

Dianna is pushing my transport chair as fast as she can walk, but the door to the parking lot is about a third of the mall away. I am trying hard to keep the coat on my lap to conceal the fact that my pants are at about mid-thigh. Our Christmastime impromptu shopping trip with our children, who brought their families to Tennessee to spend Christmas with us, is not going well.

I can't help but notice the stares from other shoppers. I can't tell if the looks on their faces indicate curiosity or disapproval. A quick check of the coat I'm using as a covering reveals the reason for their stares, the coat has shifted and a portion of my bare thigh is exposed.

How did I get in this situation, careening down Opry Mills Mall, Nashville, Tennessee during the Christmas rush with my pants down, fighting hard to hold back the tears? (See Chapter 9 for the rest of the story.)

"MS is a sneaky disease." That's how one medical professional described multiple sclerosis. Her point, at the time, was that things change. What is true today in terms of symptoms may not be true tomorrow. What works today in terms of coping may not work tomorrow. My journey with MS has been long and varied. In the early days, there were many times when I could forget I had the disease. As the years rolled on it became harder to ignore. Today I rarely forget that I have MS. If I do, I need only to try to move to remind myself.

Physically, it has been like an encroaching darkness. It began with only a thin shadow over 25 years ago. I didn't have a name for it then; I just knew something wasn't right.

Part 1 of this book roughly chronicles the progress of this disease in my body. Frankly, it was uncomfortable to write. I have journals for some of those years, but my vision difficulties and the poor legibility of my writing, which has grown worse over the years, have combined to make a strict chronology impossible.

I am very aware that my story is not unique or particularly striking. Many others with MS, and a host of other diseases, have suffered much more. I don't present this to make you feel sorry for me, but to provide context for what I have to say in Part 2.

My story is simply an account of the faithfulness of God, but it makes much more sense if you understand the journey. Walk quickly through the darkness for there is hope at the other end.

# Chapter 1

## The Journey Begins

It was a tingle. Nothing more. It ran up the back of my legs. There was no pain. There was no weakness. Nothing to cause alarm.

In February of 1981, at 22 years of age, I became a pastor. I was too young, and still in college. But after filling the pulpit for a tiny church whose pastor had resigned, the church leadership decided I was ready to take the helm of the First Free Will Baptist Church of Tulare, CA. A year or two later, concerned about how sedentary I had become since accepting the pastorate, I had decided to walk every day at lunchtime. The walk was only a mile or so, but it was invigorating and made me feel like I was doing something good for myself.

I had always been active when I was younger. I played baseball in elementary school, basketball in high school on lower-level teams and two years at a small college I attended. As a teen and young adult I spent countless hours playing pickup basketball, city league softball, bowling in a league, and as my father-in-law said, "Playing anything with a ball."

Before becoming a pastor, my previous work experience had always been some form of physical labor. As a teenager, I worked in restaurants, usually as a dishwasher or busboy. As a college student, I worked for a trucking line, handling heavy boxes.

Just prior to entering the pastorate, I spent more than three years working at Sandpointe, a plant that built mobile homes. There, I spent my days installing water heaters, conducting gas line checks, doing linoleum patches, loading furniture, and fulfilling various other responsibilities.

Now as a pastor, I was spending hours in study and sermon preparation, visiting the sick and shut-in, counseling young believers, leading worship, conducting funerals, etc. My lack of vigorous physical activity was taking a toll on my body and adding a little more around the middle.

The post-walk tingle in my legs was something similar to what one feels when receiving TENS stimulation from a physical therapist or chiropractor. It definitely got my attention, but since there was no pain, I saw no reason to address it with a doctor. Besides, I wasn't interested in creating a doctor's bill we couldn't afford. Looking back, it was step one on a long journey.

Those were busy years. We had two small children, a first grader and a toddler. I was doing my best to be an involved father, taking night classes in an effort to finish my degree, pastoring a small but growing congregation, and dreaming of ministry "success", whatever that is. I didn't have time to address an inexplicable tingle that lasted only a few minutes and occurred only at the end of a long walk.

After some four years as the pastor of that church, I accepted the challenge of moving to the other end of the state in hopes of planting a new church in Sacramento,

California. After several months of fundraising, I moved my young family to the big city over New Year's holiday in 1986. I was filled with the kind of confidence that comes from ignorance. Professionally, I had no idea what I was getting into. My wife, Dianna, and I were entering the most stressful time we had experienced in our young marriage.

Our brief foray into church planting would last only 18 months. The church never got off the ground for a variety of reasons. I could say it was a result of not having a good place to meet, a lack of partners that would assist in the work, and a host of other things. But the biggest problem was that I didn't possess the skill set necessary for the work.

However, within the first few months in Sacramento I developed a pain that seemed to come from my right eye. The pain was serious enough that I went to a doctor. After a brief examination she wasn't certain about the cause, but felt that I might have pulled a muscle (although she had no idea how) that was causing my pain. She told me to go home and try some ice and Advil, then come back if it didn't help. It didn't.

Instead of getting better, things got worse. I noticed deterioration in my vision in that eye. At first, things were just a little blurry. But soon I found I could not read the headlines on the newspaper out of my right eye. Once, while driving at night I closed my left eye and couldn't make out the freeway lanes. Worse yet, I was noticing a black spot in my vision. Now I was more concerned. My vision had always been excellent but now it seemed to worsen by the day. I made an appointment for a follow-up with the doctor.

On my return visit, she still didn't have any answers, but she was concerned enough to refer me to an ophthalmologist at the University of California at Davis. After much more extensive examination he informed me that what I had was retrobulbar optic neuritis. He explained that this was swelling of the optic nerve behind the eye. It causes a distortion in the vision and often a black spot in the field of vision.

"What do we do about it?" I asked.

"Normally, we do nothing. This kind of thing usually resolves itself over about six to eight weeks. If it doesn't resolve itself we treat it with steroids, but we like to avoid that if we can."

Before I left they scheduled me for a follow-up visit in two weeks. I went home, trusting the doctor to know what he was talking about. But, the next two weeks made me wonder if that were the case. In the days between those appointments my vision worsened. The faint dark spot in my vision grew larger and blacker. My concern mirrored its growth.

In that first follow-up visit, the doctor, however, seemed neither surprised nor concerned.

The ophthalmologist told my wife and me that sometimes, but not often, optic neuritis results in the complete loss of vision in the affected eye. We were stunned.

"But what if he loses the vision in that eye?" Dianna questioned.

"Then he'll be a guy with *one* eye," replied the doctor. "There are millions of people that only have vision in one eye."

The doctor's words were meant to be encouraging, but I didn't find them to be so. Another appointment for two weeks later was made and we left with more than a little trepidation.

Thankfully, the next two weeks were better. Vision in the affected eye slowly began to improve. By the follow-up appointment, the black spot in my vision had shrunk slightly. After another month, it was gone altogether.

The day the doctor released me, Dianna and I were feeling pretty good. Things had gone as well as could be expected until the doctor gave us one last thing to think about.

"There is one thing you need to know about optic neuritis that we haven't discussed. Optic neuritis is sometimes the first symptom of multiple sclerosis. And you are about the right age when MS manifests itself. If this should ever return it will be important for you to find a doctor soon."

Needless to say, his words were sobering, but they didn't give me pause. I was young (mid-twenties) and strong, and unconcerned about something that might or might not occur in the distant future.

In hindsight, I can recall another incident during that timeframe in Sacramento that may have been a window into my future struggle with multiple sclerosis.

A good friend, Jim McClelland, invited me to join his church's team in a basketball tournament in Fresno. Jim and I had played a lot of sports together, so I eagerly agreed, even though I had not been playing regularly. With a basketball goal mounted on my garage, I went out to practice a bit.

**FROM JONATHAN'S JOURNAL:**
*10/21/98 "Fatigue grips my body like a vice today. I need Your strength. There is much to do today and I cannot do it on my own."*

One thing led to another, and I ended up in a game with two post-college neighbors. I told them about my past experience with basketball and that I was getting ready for a tournament. (Actually, I was bragging a bit.) But when we began to play, I looked more like an old man who thought he was better than he was and couldn't keep up with the young guys — in spite of the fact that I was only a couple of years older.

I knew I was out of shape. And I knew my shot was rusty. What I didn't expect was the weakness in my hands.

I found it difficult to catch the ball or grab it for a rebound. The ball went through my hands like water. A couple of weeks later, when I played in the tournament, I had the same difficulties. Again, I knew I wasn't in basketball shape but I sensed something else was wrong.

Early in 1987, my world was about to be rocked again. The tiny church continued to struggle and we lost some faithful attenders. (We had already been forced by economic realities to meet in a poor facility and location.) "Discouraged" does not begin to describe how I felt.

Out of the blue, at least from my perspective, I received a call from a leading member of our sponsoring board. He told me of his plan to leave the church he pastored in Garden Grove, CA. To my surprise, he asked if I would be interested in replacing him. I was stunned.

I had sensed that the board had given up on me; now I knew it to be the case. This man had always treated me well and had been a source of encouragement. If he thought it was time for me to pull the plug on the work in Sacramento, I knew the rest of the board felt the same way.

So after brief discussions, and a long-overdue week of vacation, I became the pastor of the Garden Grove Free Will Baptist Church. But, while I left the failed church plant behind, my health issues were just getting started.

A year or two after I had moved my family to Garden Grove, I woke up with an old familiar pain in my right eye. Remembering the words of the ophthalmologist at UC Davis, I knew it was time to look for a local eye doctor. Our new primary care physician made a recommendation. I made an appointment.

This new ophthalmologist came with impressive credentials. According to his office walls he had won many awards and been recognized, at least by some, as a leader in the field. Frankly, I found him to be rather condescending and a bit of what my Mom would call a "smart aleck." He seemed unconcerned about the recurrence of optic neuritis. Although he acknowledged that it had returned, he said little else. A follow-up visit was scheduled for several weeks later.

Just as it had previously, the optic neuritis resolved itself in a matter of weeks. A few months later, I had another similar episode. Once again, the ophthalmologist's conclusion was that it was optic neuritis. Like the other incidents, it resolved itself in a few weeks.

What really got my attention though was when it showed up again, only this time in my left eye. This time, I did a little research before going to the doctor and read that optic neuritis doesn't normally move from one eye to the other. So when the ophthalmologist diagnosed optic neuritis my left eye, I had a question for him.

"I've been doing some reading and some of the authorities say optic neuritis doesn't usually occur in both eyes or move from one eye to the other. So what does this mean that I've now had it in both eyes? "I asked.

The doctor seemed offended by my question, dismissing it flippantly saying, "It means you are one in a million." A moment later he left the room.

I was angry, but decided there was no use in arguing with him. I went home and made an appointment with my primary care doctor. At that appointment, I explained my frustration with the ophthalmologist. My primary care doctor said, "Maybe it is time that you see a neurologist about a neurological problem rather than ophthalmologist."

I agreed and she gave me the name of a neurologist in nearby Santa Ana, CA. But, before I left her office, she concluded our visit with some ominous words, "If this is MS, you will need to make some preparations." Her words washed over me like a cold wave. It was the first time I had heard a doctor warn about what the future might hold for me.

# Chapter 2

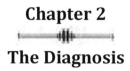

# The Diagnosis

My first visit with Dr. Goldman, the neurologist, provided few answers. Younger than I expected, but seemingly quite knowledgeable, he said it could be MS but it was probably too early to tell. He did suggest, however, that I have a Magnetic Resonance Imaging of the brain and that might provide a better answer. The MRI was scheduled for a week or so later at a local hospital.

I never really knew I was claustrophobic until I had an MRI of the brain. I do remember crawling under the house once as a kid with my dad to "help" him fix something and thinking, *if someone blocks that little hole we used to crawl under here, we're going to be trapped!* But in the presence of my superhero dad my fear only lasted a few seconds.

When I entered the MRI room, the technicians seemed distracted. It didn't help that the MRI machine was located in what looked like a mobile home in the hospital parking lot. (Keep in mind, MRI was still a new technology then and older hospitals were still finding places to house it.) The technician told me the MRI would create lots of noise, but cause no pain. In fact, it would be over with in about 20 minutes. Since no one seemed concerned about anything, I decided there was nothing to be concerned about. I was wrong.

They first had me remove all metal from my body (wristwatch, wedding ring, coins in my pockets, etc.), quizzed me about any "hidden" metal (embedded metal shavings, penile implant, etc.). Then, he inserted earplugs in my ears and laid me on a cold hard table. They covered my eyes with a washrag, strapped down my head and my arms, and then pulled a plastic hood or helmet over my face. They slid me into the tube headfirst until only my feet were exposed. As they slid me inside, I had to scrunch my shoulders to fit in the tight tube.

Once I was inside, the noise began. It started as a quiet knocking and then grew louder, much louder. The noise was aggravating, but much less disconcerting than my imagination. Remembering that I lived in Southern California, where earthquakes were a common occurrence, I began thinking *what happens if we have a big earthquake while I'm in here? How will I get out? My hands are strapped down. I don't trust those guys to get me out. Besides, they might be injured and unable to take care of me. There's no doubt I would survive even a major quake, I'm surrounded by metal, but I'd be stuck in here!* I had read stories of people being trapped in the rubble days after earthquake.

Soon, my heart was racing . . . and I was hearing voices . . . it was the guys in the control room trying to talk to me on the intercom. "Jonathan, you seem to be a little anxious. Take it easy and try to relax. This will be over before you know it." But it was much too late for me to take it easy. Instead, I began to pray and quote all the Scripture I could remember.

True to their word, after about 20 minutes (in retrospect, it turned out to be the briefest MRI I have ever had) they slid me out of the tube, removed the "hood", and unstrapped me. I was so shaken, I didn't even hear what they said. All I wanted was out!

After my heart rate returned to normal on the drive home, I was embarrassed. There was nothing to it. The MRI didn't hurt. There was no reason to be afraid. I was in no danger, but I was scared to death. I consoled myself with the thought that I'd never have to do that again. Little did I know that in the years to come I would have many more MRI's. Few would be as simple as the first.

My distress was only heightened when I met with the neurologist a few days later. He explained that MRIs are a good diagnostic tool for MS, but sometimes they don't provide enough information for a diagnosis. In my case, the MRI showed no plaques (lesions) in my brain, a telltale sign of MS. Without those, a diagnosis was difficult. His plan, was to wait and see. He instructed his staff to make me a follow-up appointment about three months later. I left there frustrated with the lack of answers.

As I walked toward my car, I remember silently praying, *Lord, I still don't know what the future holds, but I know You do. I guess I'll just keep trusting You.* Proverbs 3:5-6 came to mind: "Trust in the Lord with all your heart and lean not on your own understanding; in all your ways submit to him and he will make your paths straight."
The timing of that follow-up appointment would prove providential. A few days before the appointment I was

playing the piano and noticed that my left hand did not seem to work well. I've never been a great pianist, but I have played for my enjoyment and occasionally at church. Yet, even allowing for my ineptitude, I could tell something just didn't seem right.

When I told my neurologist about my perceived weakness at my follow-up appointment, he frowned and checked my hand. He said he didn't notice any abnormalities, but we would continue to watch it. I left his office knowing no more than I did when I came.

My next follow-up appointment was scheduled for three months later, but that changed when I woke up one morning and the bed sheets didn't feel "right" on my lower legs. It was as if I was wearing some kind of leggings or long underwear. My lower legs were not numb, but they lacked normal sensitivity and felt swollen even though they weren't. I called the neurologist's office for an earlier appointment.

It took a few days for them to get me in, and by that time the strange feeling had expanded to include everything from the waist down. The neurologist seemed more interested now. He poked and prodded and determined that I had indeed lost some sensation. I felt better knowing that I wasn't imagining things.

His exam completed, the doctor reminded me that sometimes evidence of multiple sclerosis doesn't show up on MRI, but before a doctor can make a diagnosis of multiple sclerosis he or she must see evidence of the disease in more than one portion of the body. With this latest episode, he had seen evidence of MS in three sectors of my body: my eyes; my arm; and now my legs. "I feel very confident," he said, "that I can say with some certainty that you have multiple sclerosis."

Dr. Goldman was quick to reiterate what he had said about MS on other occasions. Having the diagnosis did not mean I would ever be confined to bed or in a wheelchair. Many people, he said, who have MS find it to be more of an inconvenience than a cause of debilitation. Due to early diagnosis (a result of MRI technology) and the effectiveness of new medications, this is especially true for those with the relapsing/remitting form of the disease. (At this writing, medication specifically targeting the progressive forms of the disease is just beginning to come to market.)

It was an overcast spring day when I left the doctor's office. I remember feeling relieved that I finally had an answer for the strange things I was experiencing. At the same time, I had uncertainty about the future. That day, I did what I would do many times thereafter. I said, "Lord, I don't what the future holds, but I know You won't take me down any roads where You don't go with me. I don't understand what You are doing, but I trust You." I tried hard to mean it. I was 34 years old.

Returning home, Dianna and I discussed the diagnosis at length. Both of us acknowledged a degree of fear, but we decided to trust what the doctor said and place our confidence in the goodness of God. We would worry about the other stuff when and if it became an issue.

# Chapter 3

## The Reality Sets In

Later that spring, I would discover one of the more maddening symptoms of MS: bladder incontinence. Our entire family was involved in Little League baseball at that time. I managed a team in the minor division, Dianna was a scorekeeper, and our son, Taylor, played on the team I managed. (A season or two later our daughter, Cassie, played Little League baseball as well.)

A little explanation. Taylor is actually our son's middle name. Later, in college, he chose to go by his first name Joseph. Most of his friends today know him as Joe.

Part of our responsibility as minor division managers and coaches was to umpire in the major division (ages 10-12). Some managers and coaches in the minor division disliked umpiring, but I rather enjoyed it.

In one particular game, I was umpiring first base, when I realized that I needed to use the restroom. The restrooms were in the nearby school building, and I didn't want to disrupt the game just so an umpire could go to the restroom. I decided to wait until after the game. As the next inning began, however, I realized I was in trouble.

The urge to go suddenly was much worse. I began to panic. I couldn't leave in the middle of the inning. But the urge was more intense than anything I had ever felt. I shifted back and forth. I turned away from the stands as much as possible. Then, after two quick outs, I began to feel urine dripping down my leg.

The final out of the inning was a pop fly and as soon as it hit the glove I started running for the restroom. When I finally got there I was glad to discover that I hadn't emptied my bladder entirely. Due to the fact that my pants were dark blue the wet spot was hardly visible in the mirror. I had read about MS causing bladder incontinence in some people, but now I was beginning to realize what that was all about. I decided to just stay away from the stands and to leave immediately after the game.

I went home that day determined to be more careful. I had a few close calls in the following days, but then the problem seemed to go away. I tried to put MS out of my mind.

A few months later, another experience brought MS to the forefront. Living only a few miles from the ocean, our family enjoyed walking on the beach, looking for shells and exploring tide pools. This was especially true in the winter months, when we would often have the beach all to ourselves. One such day led us to Pelican Point, south of Newport Beach. We had a great time laughing, walking along the beach, exploring, and climbing along the undeveloped shoreline. It was cool and overcast, so we were alone on the beach.

After several hours of climbing and walking, I was tired, but not extraordinarily so, when we started up the asphalt service road toward the parking lot and our car. The service road was steep, used only by Rangers and beach patrol. It was gated at the top so not just anyone could drive a car down it.

As we walked, however, I began to feel an intense fatigue. In a matter of moments, my legs felt like stone. I could no longer feel my feet. It felt like my legs were stumps and my feet were in buckets of cement. It seemed all I could do to put one foot in front of the other to take a step. I was frightened and confused. What was going on? Was I having a stroke? Was I imagining it all or is this how MS advances, suddenly you lose the ability to walk?

Recognizing my distress, Dianna took hold of one hand, my daughter, Cassie, took the other hand, and my son pushed me from behind. Slowly, we began to plod our way up the hill at what seemed like a snail's pace. My legs felt heavy and lifeless, like tree stumps. Frustration, fear, and embarrassment bubbled up inside me, and I began to cry. For the first time, I think, my children realized that all was not well with Dad.

A whirl of emotions spun through my head on the drive home: fear; embarrassment; dread; anger; etc. I wondered if I would ever regain strength that was lost. But, after a 30-minute drive home I was feeling much better. Though I was very tired, when I arrived home I seemed no worse for the wear.

I had learned important lessons. First, a rise in body temperature worsens MS symptoms temporarily. We had made a somewhat long walk to the beach, like you would make from the far reaches of the parking lot and to the store, and we had played along the beach for some time. Although it was a cool day, I was dressed relatively warmly and my body temperature had gone up. When I started up the steep incline I began to notice my fatigue, but I didn't recognize it on level ground.

Second, I was reminded that heat-related symptoms get better when you cool off and rest. My lifelong love of warm weather was going to have to change. I had been known to play basketball for hours outdoors in 100° weather when I was in high school. I enjoyed working in the yard in the summer heat. I took pride in never letting the heat determine my schedule. All that had to change.

Third, I learned that my struggles had a powerful impact on those who love me. Dianna and our children were as scared as I was. Unlike my difficulties at the baseball field, they saw it all. There was no downplaying it or laughing it off.

Another incident that got my attention in those early days also occurred on the baseball field. I was conducting the practice for my Little League major division team (a year or two after the umpiring incident), in particular, throwing for batting practice. I was a pitcher when I played Little League, so I enjoyed throwing batting practice.

I was throwing for one of the better hitters on our team. He had a lot of natural ability and was spraying line drives all around me. Suddenly, he rocketed one of those line drives right at me. I saw the ball as it left the bat, but it disappeared from my vision almost instantly. The next time I saw it was after the ball had hit me in the upper left arm. It hurt, but nothing broken. I did have a nasty bruise to remind me that MS was taking a slow but steady toll on my body. When I thought of what damage might have been done had the ball hit me in the face, I decided on the spot that my days of pitching batting practice were over.

It was about that time my neurologist talked to me about DMT (Disease-modifying therapy). This is a drug regimen designed to alter the course of the disease. These drugs were still relatively new. At that time, there were two major DMTs for the treatment of MS: Avonex and Betaseron. Both were self-injections, both had shown some degree of effectiveness in trials.

**FROM JONATHAN'S JOURNAL:** *3/14/96*

*"No whining today, Lord. Problems, I have no shortage of, but there is also no shortage of Your grace and power to deal with problems. Thank You for teaching me so much of late."*

The neurologist told me of a trial that was taking place involving Betaseron for the treatment of secondary progressive MS. He thought it might be a good opportunity for me to get top-rated treatment at the University of California at Irvine at no cost to me.

This may be a good place for me to explain the three major forms of MS. Understand that I'm not a neurologist and I'm speaking in layman terms according to my own understanding of the disease.

There are three primary forms of multiple sclerosis: relapsing-remitting MS (in which patients experience relapses or exacerbations for a period of days or weeks and then return to where they were prior to the relapse), secondary progressive MS (which may include relapses, but they result in progressive worsening, a downhill slope in functionality), and primary progressive (which is not characterized by relapses, but rather a steady downhill trend usually resulting in severe disability).

Because relapsing-remitting MS is the most common form, it has received the most attention from drug makers. In addition, experts say that the progressive forms of MS are really a "different animal," rather than merely being a worse form of relapsing-remitting. What works on relapsing-remitting often proves ineffective on the progressive forms.

To complicate matters a little more, there was also debate at the outset regarding how to measure the effectiveness of the drugs. MS is a neurological disease. In other words, it has to do with the nervous system. Simply put, MS attacks the nerves in the brain by damaging the myelin sheath that encompasses the nerve like insulation covers a wire. As a result, the nerves misfire sending wrong signals (or no signal at all) to various portions of the body. This results in extreme fatigue, odd sensations, loss of normal function of limbs, vision problems, bladder/bowel incontinence and/or constipation, loss of balance and ultimately causes various types of disability.

This activity shows up in MRIs of the brain as plaques or lesions. People with MS may have one or more plaques in various portions of the brain. The location and size of these plaques determines what portions of the body are affected. As a result, MS can affect many portions of the body.

The effectiveness of a DMT is measured by a reduction in the number or size of plaques in the brain. However, there is not necessarily a connection between the number or size of plaques in the brain with a degree or nature of disability.

As one neurologist explained to me, when the DMT "disease-modifying drugs" were first being tested they needed a means of measuring their effectiveness. Since disability is somewhat subjective, they decided to use the number and/or size of plaques in the brain as the ruler by which the effectiveness of the drug would be measured. Thus, researchers measured the drugs on a basis that is different from that which most MS patients would measure them.

That is not to say that these expensive drugs are ineffective. The DMTs have made a great difference in the prognosis of the newly diagnosed MS patient as compared to those in previous decades. For many people with MS today, the disease is far more of an inconvenience than a debilitating condition.
Yet, all of the DMTs have some degree of side effects. The side effects range from nausea and flu-like symptoms to PML (Progressive Multifocal Leukoencephalopathy), a rare brain infection that often results in severe disability or even death. Some patients actually say the side effects of the various MS treatments are worse than the disease.

The patient's response to a particular drug is highly individual.

As my neurologist expected, I was accepted into the drug study of Betaseron's effectiveness in the treatment of secondary progressive MS. It was a double-blind study (a study in which neither patient nor the physician knows who is getting the drug and who is getting a placebo), I would not know if I was receiving the drug or a placebo. The drug was administered through subcutaneous (under the skin) self-injections every other day. Progress was measured by frequent examinations and intermittent MRIs.

**FROM JONATHAN'S JOURNAL**: *3/13/96 "[Lord,] You saw me through one MRI. You'll see me through another. My present focus must be upon You, not my fears."*

Given my first experience with MRI, that was an uncomfortable part of the study for me. The MRIs for the drug study were much more extensive than what I had experienced before. My first MRI had been about 20 minutes. The first MRI for the drug study lasted more than an hour and a half. To make it easier for me, they gave me IV sedation. Unfortunately, they only did that for the first and second MRIs.

After the first month, I was experiencing some flu-like symptoms. The neurologists I saw during the study told me they were pretty sure that I was receiving the drug, not the placebo. (They couldn't be sure, since they were blinded for the study as well.) They did know, however, that my MRIs were not showing any new plaques.

Two years into the three-year study, they announced the study would come to a premature end. They merely told us "the study goal has been accomplished." I wouldn't find out until years later that Betaseron had proved as ineffective as a treatment for secondary progressive MS that they halted the study early.

They did offer to provide the medication free for one year for anyone who was in the study whether they were on the drug or placebo. Accepting that offer, I continued injections. When these new injections began, however, the side effects got much worse. I continued injections for about a year before the side effects, feeling like I had the flu every other day, became more than I wanted to handle.

We hadn't been in Tennessee very long before my old friend bladder incontinence made itself known again. I dropped my wife off for traffic school and left to go find myself some dinner. I noticed a slight urge to urinate and I thought I could wait, perhaps even until I got home. In a matter of moments that urge went from slight to serious. I had no choice but to find a place to go . . . NOW!

I stopped at the closest place I could find, Taco Bell, and made a mad dash to the restroom. But when I got there, the door was locked and the sign said, "Get Key from Counter."

Desperate, I ran to the counter. The worker behind the counter was in a playful mood. He looked at me with a serious expression and said, "That will cost you five dollars." I was in no mood for levity. I muttered something under my breath and reached for my wallet I quickly found a five-dollar bill and threw it at the counter.

The kid behind the counter pushed the bill back toward me and said, "I was just messing with you, dude. You don't have to pay." With that he threw the key on the counter. At the moment I reached for the key I felt warm liquid running down my leg. I almost had the key in my hand when he quickly snatched it off the counter and laughed. What ensued was a quick game of keep-away. He would put the key on the counter, I would reach for it, and he would snatch it away and laugh.

At that moment, I was ready to come across the counter and make him eat that key! I said, "I don't think you're funny." He got the idea that I wasn't amused and he meekly handed me the key. I hurried toward the bathroom, thinking *I hope he has to clean the floors. If so, he'll know that I wasn't kidding.*

In the bathroom, I assessed the damage. I had one wet sock, a dripping leg, a distinctive aroma of urine, and a much bruised ego. I did the only thing I could do, I patted down the wet spots with paper towels and hurried to my car, vowing to be more careful in the future and never to enter that Taco Bell again. In the days ahead, there would be more such incidents, but I would be more careful about going to the restroom in time.

Thankfully, the lack of control came and went over the ensuing years. I say thankfully because some MS patients end up with an indwelling catheter and a bag strapped to their leg. In the days ahead, my problem would be an inability to empty the bladder, resulting in recurrent urinary tract infections (UTIs).

# Chapter 4

## A Grinding Fatigue

Perhaps the most frustrating symptom in the early days and still today is what some have called "a grinding fatigue." I struggle for words to describe this. It's unlike any fatigue I ever experienced prior to MS. A good night's sleep, a change of pace, or even a few days off won't resolve it.

> **FROM JONATHAN'S JOURNAL:**
> *2/10/96 "Sometimes, Lord, this disease drives me crazy. I hate being weak. I feel helpless. Sometimes I feel cheated. Often, I feel like a burden to others. However, in spite of the problems and frustrations, I must say to you, Lord, that my life is good."*

Everybody gets tired. You go for a long run or you have a killer workout at the gym and you get tired, but that's a good tired. You feel a sense of accomplishment, like you have done something good for yourself.

Or, you have a long day at the office or the kids have been fussy all day and you stumble in the door after work or you put the kids down for the night and flop into the recliner or bed, breathe a huge sigh of relief, and say, "What a day! I am exhausted!" We all know what that feels like. That is fatigue.

The grinding fatigue of MS seems different to me. Perhaps the best way I can explain it is to liken it to the process of preparing pasta by boiling it in water. When you put pasta noodles into boiling water for a short time, they get soft and pliable, ready for sauce, cheese, meat, and whatever else you want to add to make a delicious meal.

MS fatigue is more like what happens when you leave the pasta in the boiling water too long. After a long while in the water, the pasta begins to breakdown, fall apart, and turn mushy. No matter how much sauce, cheese, or meat you add, it is not going to be an attractive serving or a tasty dish.

MS fatigue leaves you feeling like that over-boiled noodle, broken down, falling apart, and mushy. It can be brought on by stress, over-activity, or nothing at all. Sometimes you can pinpoint the cause (I tried to do too much yesterday), but other times there seems to be no rhyme or reason (I don't know why I feel this way, I just woke up like this).

I think the first time I felt this kind of fatigue was climbing the hill at Pelican Point. As noted previously, it felt like my legs were stumps and my feet were in buckets of cement. On one hand, I could say I had been physically exerting myself for a couple hours, walking on the beach, playing on the cliffs, etc. On the other hand, I was still in pretty good shape and I wasn't doing anything I hadn't done a dozen times before. On that day, I regained strength rather quickly, at other times it has been exceedingly slow to return.

What is the cause of this fatigue? No one really knows for sure, but it is generally accepted that it is due to the nervous system having to work so hard because it is compromised. Even the very natural things we do — standing up, sitting down, taking a bath or shower, walking out to the mailbox, or just buying groceries — can leave the MS patient limp as a dish rag.

This is extremely difficult for those who love the MS sufferer. It means that plans made weeks in advance can crumble at the drop of a hat. Even events the MS patient has been looking forward to may become impossible. This is frustrating for the patient as well as their friends and/or family.

Quite often, the people around the MS sufferer are frustrated. Their frustration can lead to demeaning comments or even accusations of "faking it." In my experience, no one is more frustrated than the MS patient.

**FROM JONATHAN'S JOURNAL:** *10/6/10 "Father, my physical and emotional state is wearing on me. I do not feel well — shaky, achy, cold-then-hot, always on the verge of spasms, so it seems. Emotionally, I'm battling irrational fears, a deep sense of inability, and a loss of confidence and self-assurance."*

To make matters worse, some of the medications used to treat MS or its symptoms make the fatigue even greater. There have been many times when I've been looking forward to something only to discover that I cannot do it, at least not on that particular day. There are, of course, medications that can help with fatigue. However, it is a precarious balance between taking enough of the medication to offset the fatigue without making it impossible to rest or sleep.

For me, at least, this fatigue is often triggered by an elevation in body temperature. Many MS patients are heat sensitive. A hot room, a parked car on a sunny day, or even a hot bath can trigger this fatigue. This became clear to me on an overnight getaway with Dianna.

We have always made a point to invest in our relationship by taking an occasional overnight trip, even when our kids were young. I've always felt it was money well spent and time well invested. We are particularly fond of Jacuzzi suites. One of our favorite spots when we lived in California was a hotel in Fullerton, just a few miles from our home, where every room was a Jacuzzi suite.

I had always been a fan of hot baths and as we filled the Jacuzzi on one winter night I was looking forward to sliding into the warm water. It felt as good as I thought it would and we spent the next 45 minutes or so relaxing, talking, and enjoying the water. When it came time to get out, though, my legs were weak and shaky and my vision was impaired by the same symptoms I had with optic neuritis.

With Dianna's help, I got out of the Jacuzzi and lay on the bed. As I lay there, I realized that I was totally drained. I could hardly lift my legs or my arms. What's wrong with me? Why am I so exhausted?

It was then that I remembered something I read or heard: sensitivity to heat among MS patients is so prevalent that in the days before MRI, MS was actually diagnosed by immersing the patient in a tub of hot water. If the patient emerged from the water completely exhausted and wrung out, the diagnosis was made.

A physician whose wife had MS told me she was only comfortable when temperatures were between 70 and 73°. I've never put a figure on it, but I do think most MS patients would agree that we have a narrow range of comfort that generally falls in those parameters. (Oddly, cold temperatures are debilitating in a different way, exacerbating spasticity and causing muscle spasms.)

This temperature sensitivity can make conditions that are slightly uncomfortable for the average person entirely intolerable for the person with MS. Simple things like sitting in the draft of a commercial air-conditioner or next to windows where the sun is beaming in can turn an enjoyable concert or meal into an exercise of endurance, at the least.

The last time we tried a Jacuzzi suite, we kept the water temperature cooler, but I still couldn't get out on my own. So we tried an experiment, draining the tub of hot water and replacing it with cold water. After a few minutes, my body temperature was back to normal and I could get out

FROM JONATHAN'S
JOURNAL: *4/20/96*
*"Today's a bit
frustrating – a lot to
do, a lot of fatigue, and
to top it off pigeons in
the sanctuary... again!
(Twice in one week!)
But, I am reminded
how piddly my
problems are — if only
such things were the
worst of mankind's
problems."*

on my own. Our experiment worked, but it was hardly the romantic evening we had anticipated.

After moving to Tennessee in 2002, I discovered that cold weather also has a dramatic effect on MS patients. The cold causes muscles to knot up and stiffen to the point of pain. When I'm cold, I'm miserable.

None of this may seem like a big deal to the average person, however, we're not talking about a mild difference of opinion regarding where to set the thermostat. Even minor changes in temperature can be debilitating to the to an MS patient.

Think of all the places you go: restaurants, theaters, athletic events, outdoor picnics, your friends' homes, church, stores, doctors' offices, etc. Temperatures can vary significantly in those venues. Those differences can determine whether an event is feasible or not, the great difficulty is that you don't always know the circumstances until you arrive. This sensitivity may not be the worst of MS symptoms, but it is the one that most often keeps me at home.

Even when I was fully ambulatory, my temperature sensitivity forced me to give up or dramatically scale back many activities. It's hard, for instance, to umpire a baseball game when the sun comes out and warms you up because my visual acuity is the first thing to go when I get too warm. You can't call what you cannot see.

Fatigue also makes recovery from other problems tougher. For example, having a cold or the flu is uncomfortable for anybody, but a fever is more than a little disconcerting to an MS patient. Not only do you have the fatigue that goes along with the cold or flu, you also have that which accompanies a rise in body temperature. Not only do you have to deal with struggle to get back up to full speed after the illness, you have to fight this debilitating fatigue.

To the observer, it seems like "it's always something." Friends and family lose patience and quit trying to schedule things to do together. It's just easier not to include the MS patient. Conversely, the person with MS feels like he or she is a burden to the others. Unfortunately, the situation serves to isolate the patient from the people that can be the most help and encouragement.

# Chapter 5

# Collateral Damage

When I came to my senses I was sprawled across the bathtub, shower curtain beneath me shower rod on top of me. Dianna came running in to see what was causing all the noise. "Are you okay? What happened? How did you end up in the tub? Are you hurt?" My answer to her every question was the same, "I don't know."

It began a few weeks earlier, with an effort to treat my rising blood pressure. Unfortunately, I apparently inherited the tendency to high blood pressure from my mother. In my early 30s, my doctor felt it was serious enough to treat with medication and she prescribed a beta blocker.

My doctor's office was increasingly busy. She had recently been appointed as Chief of Staff at the local hospital, Garden Grove Medical Center. The influx of new patients had resulted in the hiring of a physician's assistant (PA). Simple cases like my high blood pressure had been delegated to her.

I kept returning to the office every few days while they tried to adjust the medication. Each time I had gone in my blood pressure was still high. The PA simply did the same thing the doctor would have done; she increased the dosage of the medication.

In the meantime, I had noticed that when I got up at night to use the restroom I would get some funny sensations and dizziness. It always passed quickly, so I didn't think much of it. I did mention it at the doctor's office, but they said it was probably related to my MS.

Lying in the tub, I was still out of it to a great extent, but Dianna managed to get me up and take me to the ER. There, they discovered the culprit. While the PA was increasing my medication in an effort to lower my blood pressure the medication was also slowing my heart rate. (It was in the low 30s when I arrived at the ER.)

The doctor in the ER told me to stop the medication, but warned me that the problem would not resolve itself for a day or two. He strongly suggested that I be admitted to the hospital so they could keep an eye on me. I wasn't interested. I offered a counter-suggestion: we would just keep an eye on it at home.

The doctor reluctantly agreed, noting that my heart rate had come up to about 44 in the time I had been in the ER. He let me go with a warning that if my heart rate fell below 40 I needed to return right away. I assured him that I would do so and we left.

My emancipation didn't last long. In a matter of a few hours my heart rate dipped to 37 and stayed there. Reluctantly, at least on my part, we returned to the hospital. The doctor seemed unsurprised to see me again and didn't hesitate about reminding me that I should have listened to him the first time. I humbly agreed.

In just a few minutes, they wheeled me upstairs to the room that was to be my home for the next several days. I was convinced it was all overkill until the nurse welcomed me with these words, "Mr. Yandell, I will be your nurse for the next several hours. You are in the Cardiac Care Unit. We will take good of you."

*Cardiac Care Unit? What am I doing here?* As a pastor, I had visited several people in the CCU. They were all pretty sick. *I'm not that sick. . . Wait, maybe I am . . .*

I took my confusion to the nurse, "I am in the CCU because there are no other available beds, right?"

"No, Sir," she replied, "you are here because you have a heart problem."

At that moment, I realized I was one of *them.*

I was a CCU guest for several days while the beta blocker worked its way out of my system and was replaced by different medication. What caught me by surprise was the difficulty I had in getting back to "normal" after I returned home. The whole incident left me drained and weak for almost two weeks. It was a vivid reminder that MS complicates everything.

In case I didn't get the message the first time, I later had another such reminder. With no warning, I got up one morning to discover that my right eye was nearly swollen shut and the right side of my face and neck were swollen as well. I immediately contacted the doctor and

FROM JONATHAN'S JOURNAL:
11/6/98

*"This morning, I awakened to my right eye being swollen nearly shut and the right side of my face and neck swollen as well. The doctor says she thinks it is shingles."*

made arrangements to go in that morning to see what was wrong.

To my surprise, my primary care physician took a quick look at me and announced her diagnosis: shingles. I was stunned.

*Doesn't shingles appear around the waist or torso? Isn't that something for older adults? I knew that shingles were caused by the chickenpox virus, but I had heard if you've had chickenpox you won't get shingles and I distinctly remember a two-week battle with chickenpox in first or second grade . . .*

Although what I heard was technically correct, the doctor said, some people that have had chickenpox do develop shingles, especially if they only have a light case of chickenpox. She also suggested that MS may also have opened the door for the virus by depleting my immune system.

She gave me a prescription for a medication that would help, but warned me that I might be in for a few rough days, or even weeks. She was right.

While I never had the degree of pain some people have reported with shingles (some have described it as the worst pain of their life), I did experience some significant discomfort. The swelling went down about 24 hours later but that was followed by the typical outbreak of blisters so common to shingles. I went back to the doctor a time or two over the next couple of weeks to be sure the shingles were not spreading into my eye, but mostly I just took the prescription and ibuprofen for pain. After a couple of weeks it was gone.

A few weeks later, I developed what I thought was a sinus infection. The right side of my nose was very congested and bleeding a bit, but when I tried to blow it, I would nearly be brought to tears. The pain was unlike any cold or sinus infection I ever had.

At that time, I was involved in the Betaseron drug study for secondary progressive MS through the University of California at Irvine. As it happened, I had an appointment at UCI just days after this supposed infection began. I told my neurologist at UCI about my sinus problem.

Since shingles is actually a neurological problem, rather than a skin issue, the neurologist was intrigued by this new problem. He proceeded to examine my sinuses with a small flashlight. As he did, he grunted once (a signal he had something to say) and called his nurse over to look at what he was seeing. She glanced into my nose, frowned, and cast a quizzical look at the doctor.

"That's the zoster!" he exclaimed. "That's it!" Now I was the one confused. Noting my confusion, he explained, "You have shingles," he declared, "in your nasal passages." He went on to explain that he couldn't be sure if this was a new manifestation or merely a leftover from the previous bout, but the telltale evidence of the herpes zoster was clearly identifiable.

The second round of shingles proved more painful. For the next three weeks, just touching the right side of my nose caused excruciating pain. There wasn't much to be done except to go back on the shingles medication and wait it out. After nearly a month, the tiny blisters in my nose began to disappear.

In warfare they use the term "collateral damage" to refer to destruction or loss of life that is incidental or unintentional. If a bomb dropped on the house where enemy troops are hiding and the neighbor's house is unintentionally destroyed they call that "collateral damage."

In the world of medicine, sometimes trying to fix one problem can create another. That is what happened when they tried to lower my blood pressure. At other times, one disease or medical problem can lead to another. Some of my doctors thought that was the case with my bouts of shingles. MS weakened my immune system, giving the shingles virus opportunity to manifest.

We will probably never know the full story, but we can be sure of one thing: MS complicates everything.

# Chapter 6

## Leaving Paradise

The 16 years I spent in Southern California were great for a lot of reasons, not the least of which is legendary weather. (In-and-Out Burgers is pretty high on that list, too.) Contrary to myth, it does rain in Southern California, but not too often and not too hard. By and large, SoCal has outstanding weather.

We lived in Garden Grove, in the heart of Orange County, about 8 to 10 miles from Huntington Beach, one of the most famous beaches in the world. There would normally be a few days in August that would approach 100° but the rest of the year was usually very mild. An exception might be in the fall when the hot Santa Ana winds would blow out of the desert. All in all, it was a good climate for a person with MS. So what did I do? I moved away . . . to Tennessee.

Tennessee is a beautiful state, marked by lush green vegetation. Its rolling hills of green were a stark contrast to the flat congested cities of SoCal. But I didn't go there for the natural beauty.

For about 15 years or more, I had written Bible study lessons (mostly for teenagers and their Bible study teachers) for Randall House Publications (RHP) of Nashville, Tennessee. (Randall House is the publishing arm for the National Association of Free Will Baptists, but it exists to serve Free Will Baptist churches and is privileged to serve many other like-minded churches from forty plus denominations.)

My wife and I went to dinner early in 2002 with the incoming CEO of Randall House while he was representing the company at a meeting in California. Then, one day, the Editor-in-Chief, Keith Fletcher, called again, this time about an opening for a teen editor. (The present teen editor was being promoted.)

This inquiry interested me a little because of my involvement in a teen curriculum brainstorming meeting at RHP a couple of years earlier. In that meeting we had talked about the idea of creating teen magazines that would include daily devotions that went along with Sunday's lesson. It was a rather cutting-edge concept at the time.

The editor-in-chief told me they were interested in changing the curriculum. I immediately asked if the magazine concept was on the table. If so, I felt I might be interested in talking further. If not, I had no interest in maintaining the status quo.

After being assured that it would be up to me what changes would occur, I agreed to come to Nashville for an interview. I told the folks back home I was going to Nashville to say no and put this thing to an end once and for all. I wasn't trying to fool anyone. I felt certain that they wouldn't want to do what I wanted to do. Therefore, I expected to just say no.

However, the interview went well, and to my surprise they seemed eager for me to make whatever changes I felt were best, even the magazine idea. I went back to California to pray and decide what to do. But, when the plane left the runway to return me to the West Coast, I knew in my heart I would be back. After a few days of prayerful consideration, I accepted the new position and resigned from the church in Garden Grove.

The move to Tennessee was a good professional decision for a number of reasons I won't go into here. It was not a good move for my health. One thing many people like about Tennessee is that it has all four seasons. Unlike Southern California, Tennessee has four very distinct seasons. It is cold in the winter (usually including a little snow), gorgeous in the spring, hot and humid in the summer, and pretty again in the fall. Since cold and heat are not friends to MS, I couldn't do much of anything outside except in the spring and fall.

Since we only had one car in Tennessee, a commitment we made to cut costs, when walking outdoors proved impossible due to extremes in the weather, it wasn't feasible for me to have a gym membership where I could walk indoors. Thus, my daily walking came to an end. I still miss it.

One thing about Tennessee that was very advantageous

**FROM JONATHAN'S JOURNAL:**
*7/29/06*

*"My physical condition continues to decline. Walking is increasingly difficult, as is standing for any length of time. Yet, I am learning to accept and adjust to the changes."*

was that I received extraordinary care from my first primary care physician in The Volunteer State, Dr. Paul Gentuso.

A former missionary to Cote d'Ivoire (Ivory Coast, West Africa), he understood what it was like to accept a job because you felt it was God's will, rather than because it offered a salary increase or opportunity for advancement. While I had good medical care in the past, and even now, I have never had a doctor who loved the Lord or my family as much.

For MS care, I saw (and continue to see) the head of the MS Clinic at Vanderbilt University, Dr. Subramaniam Sriram. Like the staff at UC Irvine in California, the people of Vanderbilt are on the cutting edge of MS research and treatment.

Slowly, ever so slowly, my MS began to worsen. Under the supervision of my neurologist, I tried Avonex, a weekly intramuscular interferon self-injection. I stayed with it for about a year before the side effects, feeling like I had the flu three or four days a week, became more than I wanted to bear.

Shortly before we relocated, the director (CEO) of Randall House, Dr. Alton Loveless, retired and a new director, Dr. Ron Hunter, took his place. Ron was eager and energetic and the editorial staff was tasked with the creation of an entirely new Sunday School/Bible study curriculum, which became known as CLEAR Curriculum. The launch of the new curriculum necessitated some travel from the editors as we taught customers how to use it.

(Eventually the CLEAR curriculum morphed into what is now known as D6 curriculum.)

Dianna was not employee of Randall House, but she traveled with us for many events and conducted workshops to orient teachers to the curriculum. More often, when she traveled she did workshops on teaching special needs in the church, one of her passions. (She works as the Braille transcriber for Metro Nashville Public Schools, putting print materials into Braille for blind students.)

One of the chief things she did on these trips, however, was to take care of me. I was not suffering from any debilitating weakness at that point, but I fatigued easily. I had not made a secret of my MS; the Randall House leadership had known about it and they were great at understanding my limitations.

I thoroughly enjoyed those early years at RHP. We had great fun on the road and I received great pleasure from teaching the workshops. During those early years, I also had opportunities to speak in various venues. The schedule was hectic. About once and sometimes twice a month we would be in the office Monday through Thursday, then travel and do workshops on Friday and Saturday. Our itinerary took us as far south as Florida and even north into Canada — a "wicked good" (a northern expression to describe something that is really good) trip, indeed. (That trip also introduced me to

FROM JONATHAN'S
JOURNAL: *9/9/10*
*"Father, I am struggling
with irrational fears. I
find myself to be
suspicious and doubtful
of the motives of others,
even those I know love
me. I have struggled over
the decision to take my
scooter to the D6
Conference or leave it
here. I'm fearful of taking
it because I feel it will
reinforce the general
feeling that I am
incapable of things like
the conference. Yet, I
know it might make
things easier on me.
Please give me clear
direction on this matter."*

"Putin," a tasty dish made of French fries, cheese, and brown gravy.)

While those years were good, the schedule and the climate began to take a toll on me. I hardly noticed it for a long time, but when Randall House created the D6 Conference, a yearly gathering for people committed to practicing "generational discipleship," my growing physical limitations became more obvious.

("Generational discipleship" is a term referring to one generation passing the Christian faith along to the next generation as taught in Deuteronomy 6, that's where the term *D6* comes from.)

I worked the first two D6 Conferences, but was of limited value. There was little I could do to help set up and tear down. I was using a cane occasionally and my stamina was poor. As a result, it was mutually agreed that I was not needed for the conferences, a fact that was hard for me to accept but impossible to deny.

At the first D6 Conference, I also discovered another area MS had affected: my emotions. The conference opened with a general session that gathered all the conference attendees (1000-1300 people) in one room. The air was electric with anticipation. Suddenly, the sound of drums filled the air. Turning quickly toward the sound, I saw a drum line, as might be found in a university band, marching down the aisles toward the front.

As their thunderous cadence filled the room, I was engulfed in a swirl of emotions. A lot of things were going through my mind: a sense of admiration for the conference leadership (What an exciting way to kick off an event!), a degree of pride to be involved in a small way, and even a little trepidation as I considered how the more conservative members of the denomination would feel about it.

All at once, I found myself crying. I couldn't control it. I couldn't stop it from happening. It was the first time I experienced something that has become part of my life since. My neurologist might call it Pseudobulbar Affect or PBA.

PBA is a condition that causes sudden, frequent, and uncontrollable episodes of crying and/or laughing that don't match how you feel inside. It is a distinct condition that can happen in people with a brain injury or certain neurologic conditions such as Alzheimer's disease, ALS, or multiple sclerosis.

My condition is not debilitating, but it is frustrating. I cry at the drop of a hat when anything moves me, whether positive or negative. For instance, I cry throughout most of the Sunday worship services. A tight vocal harmony, an energetic choir song, a meaningful worship song, a powerful hymn, or even good guitar solo can set me off.

It can happen at the most inopportune moments, and can include inappropriate laughter that I find impossible to control even in the saddest or most tense of moments. It is both maddening and embarrassing.

Eventually, the complications of MS forced me to leave Randall House entirely, taking early "retirement" and going on disability. In retrospect, my 15 years at what some of us affectionately called Randy's Pub (a bit of irony, since no one on staff drank alcohol) were very good. The company and its leadership were gracious, kind, and supportive. Due to policies they put in place years before, I was able to receive seven months of full salary even after I quit working. I will always be grateful for their kindness.

Without a doubt, the most difficult thing about leaving California had to be leaving our son in SoCal and my parents and two sisters, Lou Ann and Susie, in other parts of the state. (My brother, Gary, was in Texas when we moved to Tennessee but has since moved back to California.) It is difficult being so far from family, especially grandchildren! As my health has declined, it has become even more difficult.

We used to try to make the trip to California at least once a year, and go to Oklahoma to see Dianna's parents and our daughter and her family once or even twice a year. Travel is extremely difficult, however, any way one goes about it. Equally as problematic are the housing arrangements once I arrive at the destination. Homes of our family members are not handicap accessible, at least not to the extent I need.

Bladder and bowel issues have also made travel difficult. Finding a suitable place to self-catheterize was a matter of comfort when I first began to cath. However, in later years vision and dexterity issues have made it nearly impossible for me to do it alone. So the challenge now is to find a restroom where Dianna can go in with me.

Of course, a family restroom is ideal, but it must be adequately handicap accessible. We have found handicap accessible restrooms to vary greatly. Some include little more than a small angled bar on the wall to help the person to stand up from the toilet and some of these bars are so small and lightweight that they must be meant for use by 90 pound little ladies, not for 200 pound 6 foot plus men.

When you add bowel unpredictability to the mix you quickly see that travel can be tough, especially cross-country travel by car or by airplane. Of course, being able to afford the travel is another issue entirely.

I say all this simply to point out that things have not gone as we planned or anticipated. When we moved to Tennessee we envisioned frequent travel to see family. That plan has never been fulfilled.
While we enjoy the beauty of Tennessee and attend a great church and Life Group (more about that in a later chapter) the Volunteer State has been tough on us, at times. We have, however, found the people of Tennessee

are not nearly as off-putting as the weather can be, at times.

One quick example: We had just finished with lunch at Opry Mills Mall and were loading up to leave when Dianna ran into difficulty getting me into the car. I could not get out of the wheelchair and stand long enough to get turned around and seated in the vehicle. It felt as though I was tethered to the chair by a giant rubber band. We tried repeatedly, but my legs would give way and I would slump back into the chair. (This happens to me when I have been sitting in the chair for a long time or am very tired.)

Desperate, she turned to strangers walking by to ask for help. Spotting a passing group that included several young men headed toward the mall entrance, she asked, "Could you help me get him into the car?" The young men eagerly agreed and swiftly lifted me from my chair into the front passenger's seat of our SUV, proving once again that the people of Tennessee have been much kinder to us than the winter and summer weather.

# Chapter 7

## Riding the Steroid Train

After arriving in Tennessee, I also had my first experience with IV steroids. Steroids are often given to MS patients to help them get past a flare-up or exacerbation. IV (intravenous) steroids are not a cure for MS, nor are they a long-range solution for dealing with MS symptoms. However, they are beneficial for dealing with exacerbations and they provide a brief relief. They are hard on the body and overuse can cause problems. I've only taken them one time. It was quite the adventure.

I had been struggling for a while with worsening symptoms when Dianna was admitted to the hospital for surgery. While she was in the hospital, I had an appointment with my neurologist. When he learned about my worsening symptoms, he prescribed a round of IV steroids. The process included the insertion of an IV that would remain for the duration of the treatment and the first infusion in the doctor's office. I would do three or four more infusions at home on successive days.

A nurse inserted the IV while I was there in the office and I sat quietly for 15 or 20 minutes as the first dose of steroids was given. The nurse asked me two or three times if I was feeling or tasting anything unusual. She said some patients get a metallic taste in their mouth. I neither felt nor tasted anything unusual.

I had to get some lunch on the way home so I decided it would be a great opportunity to stop at one of my favorite places, Baja Burrito. I'd grown to love this place where you go through a line, tell them what you want in your burrito, and they make it for you while you watch. I made sure to get everything I wanted to make for a delicious lunch.

I found a seat and prepared to enjoy a tasty treat. I remember thinking that the only thing that could make this better would be if Dianna were there with me. After thanking God for the food, I took a big bite. Instantly, it hit me. The burrito tasted like aluminum foil! I took a quick look to be sure I hadn't accidentally bitten off a portion of the foil wrapper.

After noting that the wrapper was not missing a bite but was in fact several inches from where took a bite, I tried it again with the same result. Yuck! For a minute I contemplated taking it back, obviously they had messed up. But just before I did, I remembered what the nurse asked me about the metallic taste. Now I knew what she was talking about.

This was the burrito equivalent of what my dad used to tease us about when we were kids. If we asked for a piece of gum, he would say, "If you chew the wrapper first you'll appreciate the gum more."

I was hungry, so I managed to force myself to eat about half of the burrito. After that, I just couldn't take it anymore. I threw the rest away and left, inwardly hoping this side effect didn't stay with me for long. It was a vain hope. Nothing tasted right for about a week. I didn't realize how much I enjoyed eating until everything I ate tasted like metal. After two or three days, I concluded that this could be a good weight loss aid.

The steroids gave me an instant boost. In fact, they made me so hyper that I couldn't sleep. I had plenty of energy to deal with Dianna's hospitalization, though. I thought, "This is great! I feel like I don't even have MS."

The pharmacy gave me the successive doses in what looked like little plastic balls. I would just hook up the line from the ball to my IV and it would flow in. I did that for several days, even administering a couple of doses at work.

The negative side is steroids have some troubling side effects, one of which is not sleeping well. I didn't sleep more than 2-3 hours per night while taking them. In addition, I had a little indigestion and a little nervousness or anxiety. But, overall, the metallic taste was the most troublesome side effect I noticed. (I really enjoy eating!) It was uncomfortable, but I knew it was for a limited time.

What I didn't know was what the steroids were doing to the rest of my body. With any medication, you have to measure side effects as well as benefits. Unfortunately, I seem to be poster child for side effects.

Soon, the initial rush had ended and I went back to feeling drug out and lifeless, only now it was worse. After Dianna was released from the hospital, we both began to be concerned about my lack of energy. That's when I noticed (TMI WARNING!) my stools had become very dark, almost black. Having read someplace that such occurrences sometimes are an indicator of internal bleeding, we went to the doctor.

After listening to my story, the doctor (Dr. Paul Gentuso) did a quick test and concluded that I was indeed bleeding somewhere internally. Not only did the bleeding need to be located and stopped, but also I was in need of receiving blood. With that, Dr. Gentuso put me in a wheelchair and took me across the elevated walkway to the hospital, stopping along the way to pray with us.

This was only the third time I had been hospitalized since my birth. I spent the night in the hospital when I was in my 20s for what they called, "a spastic colon." I felt that was a nice way of saying, "You have a really bad stomach ache and we can't find any cause for it." And I had been in for several days in California when my heart rate bottomed out and I passed out in the bathroom and fell into the tub.

They began giving me blood and right away I began to regain some strength. The next day, a gastroenterologist put a scope down my throat and discovered the source of the problem – two bleeding ulcers. By then, the bleeding had stopped. There was nothing more to do. The doctor then educated me about the food (spicy, hot) and beverages (alcohol, coffee, iced or hot tea, and dark soft drinks) I should avoid. He also prescribed some medication.

When my regular neurologist heard what had happened, he added another restriction: no more IV steroids. This made my case that much more difficult to treat, sidelining one of the neurologists' favorite treatments for MS exacerbations or flare-ups.

This hospitalization also brought to light a problem I didn't know I had. I already knew I had difficulty voiding urine. For some time it had been necessary for me to "trigger" the process by pressing hard on my belly. That would be sufficient to cause my bladder to contract and expel some urine. It wasn't the best approach, but I thought it was working fine.

The diagnosis of a UTI prompted a visit from the hospital's urologist. After some preliminary tests, he thought I needed a full urological workup. That wouldn't take place until after my release. When it did take place, more tests were performed and I discovered that I was emptying only one-third of my bladder. That problem set me up for UTIs.

(One test they did at the hospital was to ask me to empty my bladder into a small container. The nurse said I would need to stand. She helped me out of bed and called another nurse to stand on the other side of me so I wouldn't fall. Then the first nurse held the container in front of me said, "Go ahead, and empty your bladder." So there I stood, between two nurses who were trying to look away while I strained to get something started. I couldn't help thinking of what a friend of mine said to me once from his hospital bed, "When you get sick, modesty goes out the window."

The lack of emptying often results in urinary tract infections (UTI). These infections are more than troublesome. When severe, they can bring on other illnesses like dementia and sepsis, often resulting in a hospital stay or even death.

After leaving the hospital I was scheduled to see a urologist for a full urological workup. They did a number of tests, but the one that interested me most is when they checked the retention level in my bladder. Using a catheter, they inserted a steady stream of liquid into my bladder with the instruction that I was to tell them as soon as I felt a strong urge to urinate.

As my bladder filled, they asked me several times if I felt the need to urinate. I replied that I did not. The longer it went on, the more concerned the nurses became. Finally, one hurried out of the room to get the doctor. The doctor came in in a rush and said, "Mr. Yandell, are you still not desperate to urinate?" Again, I replied that I was not.

"Mr. Yandell, if my bladder had as much liquid in it as yours does I would be screaming at Sarah to get it out!" He then said the same thing that was told me by the urologist at the hospital, "MS patients are supposed to have little bitty bladders that can't hold much urine, but yours is huge! It's no wonder you can't empty it on your own and it's no surprise that you have repeated UTIs."

I thought to myself, *Well, I've always been a bit of an overachiever.*

This was one area in which overachieving was not a good thing. My urologist had a better idea: self-catheterization. With that, I was turned over to a nurse who taught me how to catheterize. She also gave the name of a catheter supplier. As I left the doctor's office, it started to sink in that my life would never be the same.

The ensuing self-catheterization routine will likely last the rest of my life. Although it took a while to get used to, it does give me predictability that I didn't have before. I know I will cath five or six times a day at approximately the same time each day. That predictability eases my mind and prevents accidents.

However, in recent days as I've developed worsening double vision and less coordination and strength in my hands, I find it harder to cath on my own. As a result, I'm largely dependent upon my wife and my caregivers (all are female) to help me. This is no problem at home, but can be problematic away from home.

# Chapter 8

# The Era Closes

I rocked along with few major changes for a number of years, at least that is what I thought at the time. In reality, significant changes were slowly taking place. I walked less and used a cane almost all of the time. I catheterized six times a day, including at least one time at work. I was still struggling with constipation, but another bowel issue had my attention even more.

While I didn't have regular bowel movements, I had difficulty with a type of incontinence. Then in 2015 I began to struggle with bowel control. This exacerbated problems with constipation that I had dealt with for years. In my desperate attempt to deal with the incontinence, I created the opposite problem. To stop the diarrhea I took Loperamide (the most common brand name is Imodium®), as directed on the package. The over-the-counter drug worked as advertised, but I found myself having to use it every few days.

On the evening of June 25, 2015, I developed an increasingly severe bellyache. I had felt bloated for a few days, and had not had a bowel movement for four or five days. But that evening my belly bloated larger than ever and the pain became unbearable. I told my wife, "I have to go to the hospital." Knowing that I don't say such things lightly, she put me in the car and we headed downtown to the Vanderbilt University Hospital.

(TMI Warning!) I had been to the ER once before with severe constipation, they resolved it; first manually (yes, that was just as much fun as it sounds), then with a soapsuds enema (made more enjoyable since I'm too weak to sit on a bedpan). After a couple of hours, they sent me home. I expected the same thing this time. Instead, they did a CAT scan and determined that I had a bowel blockage. Another test revealed a Urinary Tract Infection (UTI) as well.

Needless to say, I wasn't going anywhere. They soon found me a room. I met briefly with a surgeon. He assured me that they were in no hurry to cut on me, but rather would make some attempts to resolve the problem in other ways. What I didn't know is that he had told Dianna he didn't want to do surgery because I was so weak he didn't think I would survive it. Unbeknownst to me, Dianna called the family to ask for prayer (our son Joe, our daughter Cassie, my parents, her parents, and some of our friends at church).

Over the next 48 hours, I received six enemas, several doses of Miralax, and various other similar treatments. All were ineffective and the blockage remained. I don't remember all the details because I was out of it for a good portion of the time. However, I do recall the surgeon coming in with his tablet to show me results of the CAT scan. Pointing to a spot in my bowels beyond which the bowel was very empty, he said that's where the blockage was.

I also remember what seemed like a parade of visitors. A few visitors from my job at Randall House Publications did not surprise me. Neither was I surprised that several people from our church, including pastoral staff members, stopped by see how I was doing.

I was also not surprised by our daughter being there. I knew she would be concerned, not only for me, but also for Dianna. I was shocked, however, to see my mother and father and my sister, Lou Ann, had flown in from California. I knew my parents were not fond of flying and had limited resources, and I was surprised by their arrival.

My surprise was due in large part to my ignorance of how sick I was. When my wife told me that our son, Joe, was on vacation (in Hawaii, as I later learned) but would come immediately, if needed, I got concerned.

"Am I dying?" I asked Dianna. "No," she replied. "Why would you ask that?"

"Well, it seems like you have called in the family."

"They are all just concerned about you," she explained.

I think it was the first time I ever realized how sick I was. Until then, I had been able convince myself that this was no big deal. Now I knew it was more serious than I thought.

But about the time I realized the gravity of the situation, a seventh enema brought success. The blockage gave way, and I made a thorough mess of my bed, to everyone's delight! (Except the nurses that had to clean it up, I'm sure!) A subsequent CAT scan proved that the crisis had passed.

They continued the regimen, however, except for the enemas, to be sure that I was back on track. They also continued the pain medication they started me on shortly after arriving at the hospital. As a result, I drifted in and out of sleep for a while longer.

After eight days at Vanderbilt, I was released to go home. The hospital staff recommended rehab to regain some strength, but I wasn't interested, so I went home. It was short-lived. After about five days I began talking unintelligibly and being unable to answer questions. Fearful that I had a stroke, Dianna called 911. The paramedics took me back to the hospital.

One light moment: Our daughter and her family were at our house after I came home from the first time. (All told, Cassie spent more than a month in Nashville during the hospitalizations.) Cassie, her husband Nate, and their two boys were present when the paramedics took me back to the hospital. In one of the lighter moments of that stretch, Landon (age 6 at the time) shook his finger at the paramedics and announced, "You better take good care of my Papa, or somebody is going to get punched!" They did, and no violence was necessary.

At the hospital, they did more tests and concluded that I had not had a stroke, but that I was having a severe exacerbation of my MS. MS complicates everything. I hadn't had an MRI in a while, so they decided to give me one while I was in the hospital. As I've noted previously, MRIs are more than a little uncomfortable for me. But, this one was a piece of cake since I slept through the entire scan. (I think they turned up the pain meds so it would be easy for me.)

Unfortunately, the results of the scan were not as positive. The MRI showed that I had several new lesions or plaques including two large ones, one on the left side of my brain and one on the right. The one on the right side of my brain was the largest. The one on the left side was also large, but somewhat smaller.

Since the right side of the brain controls the left side of the body (and the left side of the brain controls the right side of the body), my left side showed greater weakness than the right. Both, however, showed significant weakness in examination.

My speech was also slurred and my vision, particularly double vision, was worsened. In addition, I was having swallowing difficulties. I could not stand unassisted or transfer safely from one apparatus to another. The conclusion of the doctors and physical therapists was that I should go to rehab for a time, where I could work on rebuilding my strength a full three hours per day.

My wife and kids (home from Hawaii, Joe immediately came to Tennessee when he heard of my second hospitalization) began the search for an appropriate rehabilitation unit. They looked at a couple of possibilities, but scratched them off the list because they seemed more like nursing homes. The one they chose, TriStar Southern Hills Hospital, was excellent.

However, the whole idea had not really sunk in to me. Dianna says I was very angry at her when the ambulance took me to another hospital instead of home. I only remember being confused about where I was. My confusion was soon wiped away by the Southern Hills staff who painstakingly and repeatedly explained that I was there to rebuild my strength before I could go home.

Thankfully, as an employee of Metro Nashville Schools, my wife was on summer break. Our daughter, Cassie, agreed to stay for a while to be of help and encouragement to Dianna. No one had given me any specifics as to how long I would be there, but I was sure that working hard would mean a quicker release.

They worked me hard but not too hard, always leaving me enough energy to do the routine things like going to the toilet. Dianna and Cassie were good about coming to see me, especially in the evenings, so we could have dinner together. (A welcome respite from hospital food.)

My stay at Southern Hills lasted only two weeks. At the time of my release, arrangements were made for me to continue physical therapy at home with an occupational therapist, a physical therapist, and a nurse coming to my home.

I had become stronger in rehab and hoped to continue to grow in strength. The reality was that I grew weaker after returning home. I do not blame the therapists for not retaining or increasing my strength. I acknowledge that I wasn't as faithful in exercising as I could have been, but there was a visible worsening of my disease as well.

It was while I was home after rehab that one of the more humorous moments occurred. Someone rang the doorbell and I opened the door. Standing there was a woman I had not ever seen before. She asked, "Are you Jonathan Yandell?" When I replied that I was, she boldly announced, "I'm here give you a bath!"

Needless to say, I was stunned, but managed to stammer my way through some questions. I came to realize that she was from Care Centrex, the same organization that was supplying the physical therapist, occupational therapist, and nurse. Apparently, they had been told that I needed help bathing so they sent someone to do it. I wasn't interested in a stranger's assistance, and sent the lady on her way. It remains, however, the only time anyone ever showed up at the door wanting to bathe me.

During this time, I was trying to do a lot of things on my own. This included walking around the house, going to the mailbox, going to the toilet, self-cathing, preparing my lunch, and basically living with independence. The fact that I had people coming in and out several times each week gave Dianna some confidence as she went back to work.

I did have, however, a number of occasions when I fell. Thanks to my son, who had paid for an alert system, I was able to summon help with the button I wore around my neck. Looking back, there were several times I should've gone to the doctor or the ER after a fall. I later learned that a CAT scan I had in the hospital showed several broken ribs that healed as well as one vertebrae that suffered a compression fracture in the past.

As the falls began to mount in number and in severity, Dianna petitioned the insurance company to pay for a power chair. The chair was a recommendation from the physical therapists. She even got the doctor to write a prescription for it, but the insurance company denied it. We still felt it was needed, so we decided to pay for it out-of-pocket. To our surprise, friends from our Life Group wrote a check to cover the cost.

Thanks to Dianna's employment, I have good insurance. Yet, I am always amazed how insurance companies will deny a request for something like a power chair and end up paying for hospitalization the chair could have prevented. I guess I just don't know enough about the insurance business.

During this time, I was debating whether I could return to work. Randall House did not push me to make a decision. They left the ball in my court.

It soon became obvious that I needed help with daily living tasks such as dressing, preparing lunch, and toileting. On the recommendation of some friends we hired a caregiver, Coretta Kelsey, and her firm, Coretta Cares. Coretta and her helpers have been a tremendous asset in my care.

One day, early in the morning before the caregiver arrived, I was in the spare bedroom that we use as an office. I lost my balance, staggered back into the wall, and slid down in the floor. I wasn't hurt, but I couldn't get up and I didn't want to call the fire department. So I sat there and thought about my predicament.
I knew it was just about five or 10 minutes until my caregiver was due to arrive, so I just waited. When she came in, I called out that I was in the office and needed

help. She came in and in a matter of moments helped me to my feet.

That incident was enlightening, but not frightening. Other incidents were indeed frightening. On several occasions, I found myself lying in the floor waiting for the fire department to arrive and help me.

We have all chuckled at the TV commercial in which an elderly woman is lying on the floor and says, "I have fallen and I can't get up!" For years, I was among those who thought it was funny, but having been there and experienced that I can tell you it isn't funny. It is a particularly helpless feeling to know that there is nothing you can do but wait on someone to show up to help you.

Incidents like that, the worsening of my vision, the loss of dexterity in my fingers, my continued bladder and bowel issues, and the incessant grinding fatigue made work an impossibility.

I reluctantly faced the truth and filed for Social Security Disability. Thanks to my participation in the sick bank at Randall House, I was able receive salary until my disability payments kicked in February 2016.

I have always enjoyed working and struggled to settle in a new routine. I busied myself with preparation to teach our Life Group for a while, but I eventually found that difficult due to my vision and weak voice.

Since late fall of 2016, I have occupied myself with the writing of this volume using Dragon Naturally Speaking for Mac, a voice-to-text program. It has been a labor of love. (And if you've ever used Dragon, you will know the emphasis is on "labor.")

I miss the work at RHP, it is what I came to Tennessee to do. More important, I miss the people I worked with.

One of my most enjoyable tasks at Randall House was to introduce the new employees at the company banquet each year. I always had fun with it, often introducing them with two factual statements and one that was fictional. I might say, "This guy works in sales, but in his spare time he enjoys fishing and dressing like a princess." You get the idea.

Although I hadn't worked at RHP since June 2015, the CEO, Dr. Ron Hunter, asked me to introduce the new employees at the February 2016 banquet. I was eager to do so and thought of this as my last hurrah as a RHP employee.

On the evening of the banquet, it was cold and dripping rain. Dianna helped me dress, put me in the transport chair (similar to a wheelchair, but lighter), and began to push me toward the car. Two or three days prior she had stepped in a hole at work and hurt her knee. I knew it was still bothering her, but she said she'd be fine.

As were walking down the ramp from our front porch to the driveway, she stumbled and cried out in pain. As she was falling down, the chair slipped out of her hands and fell backward. In an instant, the chair had sailed down the ramp and flipped on its back. So there we were, Dianna slumped on the ramp in agonizing pain and me in the chair lying flat on its back.

It was dark outside, still drizzling rain, and just above freezing. Both of us were incapacitated. We both tried yelling for help, but our neighbors were not home or didn't hear. I thought about trying to roll out of the chair onto the driveway, but the only thing that would accomplish is I'd be on my belly rather than my back. I still wouldn't be able to get up.

Remembering that I had my cell phone, I decided to call 911. However, by then I was getting cold and shaking. I tried repeatedly to enter the security code on the phone but I was shaking so badly I couldn't press the numbers correctly.

Then I remembered that I could dial 911 without the phone being unlocked, but when I tried to do so I couldn't even get those numbers entered. I prayed, "God please help us!" No sooner had I prayed than my phone rang.

"This is the 911 operator," said the voice on the other end. "It appears that someone has tried to call 911 on this phone, do you need help?"

"Yes! Yes I do! I am handicapped. My wife hurt herself going down our ramp, she cannot stand and is in a great deal of pain. I am in my chair on its back in the driveway."

"I'm sending the paramedics," the voice replied. "Are you injured?"
"No, I'm not injured. But I am trapped and getting very cold."

In a few moments, paramedics arrived. They quickly set my chair upright and wheeled me into the house. They loaded Dianna into the ambulance to take her to the hospital. One of our neighbors who lived too far away to hear us yell, noticed the paramedics and came to see what was wrong. She stayed with me until a friend from church arrived.

At the hospital, they determined that Dianna had a torn meniscus in her knee. They referred her to a doctor and sent her home. She had surgery a few months later.

I was no worse for the wear after I got warmed up, but I was greatly disappointed by having to miss the banquet. Ironically, I couldn't help thinking of what the comedian Arsenio Hall had said years ago. He complained about getting a ticket that cost him over $300 for parking in a handicap spot with no placard.

Arsenio pled his case to the cop who cited him, saying, "I didn't hurt anyone! I was only in the store for a minute. Besides, it's raining out here. Handicapped people shouldn't be out in weather like this, they could slip and get hurt!"

While I disagree with his actions, Arsenio may have a point. Maybe we handicapped people should just stay home when the weather is bad.

# Chapter 9

## Where I Am Today

It began as a fun outing. For the first time in several years both our children and their families were with us for Ch1ristmas. We were having a great time being together and visiting some of the sites around Nashville. On this particular day, we took the kids and grandkids see the Opryland Hotel.

The massive hotel includes hundreds of rooms, convention space, and features three huge atriums adorned with lots of foliage, shops, and fun things like an indoor boat ride. At Christmas time the hotel is grandly decorated with thousands of lights outside and loads of Christmas decorations inside. It is impressive to even the most jaded traveler.

We strolled around the hotel for quite a while taking in the sights and sounds of the season. When we returned to our cars, the kids wanted to go to the mall next-door (Opry Mills) for some last-minute shopping. Dianna and I are not real fond of shopping, but we enjoy being with our kids and grandkids.

Once inside the mall it became apparent that I would need to use the restroom . . . soon. Someone located the family restroom little less than halfway down the mall. Dianna and I went to the restroom while the rest went shopping. However, it had been a long day and I was quite tired, too tired to stand. I struggled again and again to stand long enough for Dianna to lower my sweatpants. Long story short, by the time we got the pants down I was desperate. In my anxiety, I made a major mess in the floor.

Dianna tried to clean up the mess, clean me up and then pull my pants up. I could barely lift myself off the toilet, much less stand up, and she could not get my pants up. I was upset, she was upset, both of us were crying, the best we could do was to get me in the seat of the transport chair and cover me up as well as possible until we could get some help.

It's hard to express the frustration we both felt as we walked almost half the mall to get to the exit nearest our cars. She was walking as fast as possible and I was trying to keep myself covered, hoping that others couldn't tell that my pants, including my underwear, were at half - mast.

When we finally arrived at the exit, Dianna pulled the car up to the curb and our entourage approached it. Dianna came around on the passenger's side to help me enter the vehicle, along with my son and son-in-law. As they lifted me to my feet, they stood in a semi-circle to shield me from onlookers and pulled up my pants before lifting me into the front seat of the SUV.

I was utterly humiliated. Not only had I frustrated Dianna and myself, I had spoiled shopping for everyone. Just one more obvious evidence the disease was taking its toll on my body.

The downhill slide has continued now for some time. Most recently, my neurologist has referred me to a Parkinson's doctor. After examining me, he said I have some symptoms that are consistent with Parkinson's, but he did not want to give me that label since I already had the MS tag. (I am told there is no definitive blood test or MRI to diagnose Parkinson's, but I have clear MRI evidence of multiple sclerosis.)

To put it in simple terms, this is my reality at this writing:

I cannot walk.
I can stand only for a few seconds and I need help to do that.
I cannot go to the toilet alone, nor can clean myself after going.
I cannot fix my meals.
I cannot be left alone for more than three hours, and then only if I don't leave my chair.
I have paid caregivers with me five days a week for four hours a day.
I cannot take a bath.
I can shower only with assistance and assistive equipment.
I cannot catheterize myself.
I cannot dress myself.
I cannot get in or out of bed alone.
I cannot read a book, nor can I read much, although it is easier on computer.
I cannot type, something I used to do easily.
I can no longer play piano or guitar.
I cannot sing.
I cannot sign my name legibly.

I cannot drain my bladder except by catheterization. This is a lifelong issue.
I cannot walk across the room to hug my wife.
I cannot drive a car.
I cannot shop for birthdays, anniversaries, and holidays, except online.
I cannot make love to my wife.

It is somewhat distressing to me to list my deficiencies like this. I do so with no sense of pride or desire to engender sympathy. I am also quite aware that my situation is not nearly as bad as many others. I have friends that are in constant debilitating pain due to injury or illness. I have friends with cancer that take weekly doses of poison and suffer the physical consequences. I wouldn't trade places with any of them.

I have gone into some detail concerning my journey with MS, but I assure you this is not the end of my story. Please keep reading. You are about to enter the best part!

What I have learned on this journey has been priceless. These lessons will be the focus of the rest of this book.

# Hope
# Glows

# Introduction to Part 2

The doorways in our house have been beaten up, especially doorways to the bedroom and bathroom. That's because I'm not a particularly good power chair driver. Each doorway has marks on it where I have run into it with my chair.

Maybe it's my poor vision or lack of coordination that causes it. Then again, maybe I'm in too much of a hurry. Or perhaps, I'm just a dipstick. Whatever the reason (and all three of those reasons have their proponents), the reality is too many times when I try to go through the doorway I bang into the side, leaving another mark to testify of my lack of driving skill.

When I received a new custom-made power chair courtesy of the insurance company, I thought things would get better, but they did not. The new chair is actually wider than the old.

The wise man, however, keeps learning even from his mistakes. I like to think I'm wise, but slow. I'm getting better, but it's taking time.

The same could be said about my spiritual life. I've been at this long time. There are plenty of people and events to testify of my mistakes, but I am learning. I've been living with this rude and unpleasant houseguest called multiple sclerosis for a number of years now.

The battered doorways of my life bear silent testimony to the fact that I haven't done it perfectly.

Still, there are some lessons I have learned and that's what the section is all about. What I have learned is not particularly profound, you may even feel like you have heard it (or even *said* it) before. It's not uniquely mine, either. I'm sure others, even you, have had the same thoughts.

Nevertheless, I feel compelled to share what I believe God has taught me in this journey. Indeed, this is my whole purpose for writing this book. God has been faithful to me all along this journey in countless ways. Please allow me to share with you my story of God's faithfulness.

I cannot promise you that God will do for you exactly what he has done for me. I can promise you, based on his Word that he will be faithful no matter where the road leads.

# Chapter 10

## I Am Not Alone

Some people crave "alone time." Not me.

A stay-at-home mom with four children under the age of six desires nothing more than a little time alone. The harried businessman who spends all day answering questions, taking orders, and dealing with customers and employees, looks forward to getting some time to himself.

The individual confined to a chair, however, doesn't always feel the same as others about being alone. A fall while transferring to or from the toilet can leave you in the floor and in pain for a long time until help arrives, even if you have an emergency alert system. An unexpected stranger at the door, or even dropping a cell phone in a place you can't reach can make you more than a little uncomfortable.

The potential dangers mean that I am rarely alone. I have a caregiver with me all the time except for 2 to 3 hours of the day Monday through Friday. I have occasional visitors, delivery people, friends I talk to on the phone, social media, prayer partners, friendly neighbors, and my church family.

Yet, in spite of all these, I sometimes find myself enveloped in a shroud of fear. What if there's a fire? What if there is a tornado (a common danger in Tennessee)?

What if the power goes out? What if, God forbid, I suffer a home-invasion robbery?

As you can tell, I am pretty good at coming up with scary scenarios that could occur while I am alone. Truth be told, if I put my mind to it I can come up with a lot of reasons to be afraid. But I have found even more reasons not to fear.

As a Christ-follower, I have the promise of his presence in every circumstance of life. God has said, "Never will I leave you; never will I forsake you" (Hebrews 13:5). The writer of Hebrews continues, "So we say with confidence, The Lord is my helper; I will not be afraid. What can mere mortals do to me?" (Verse 6). The simple fact is that I'm not alone. God is with me.

This very real and personal relationship with God is the bedrock on which my life is built, from first to last. This relationship began, as I recall, just days before my fifth birthday. My father, Larkin A. Yandell, was the pastor of Central Avenue Free Will Baptist Church in Oklahoma City, Oklahoma.

I had been in church since the Sunday after I was born and faith in Christ was a natural part of our home life. Yet, even at that young age, I recognized the need to do more than go through the motions of church. I had seen many people young and old respond in the service to an invitation to come forward and pray to receive Christ as Savior.

Like most evangelical Christians, our church taught that we were all born in sin. Romans 3:23 says, "For all have sinned and fall short of the glory of God." The Bible goes on to say that the price for our sin is death, both physical death and eternal death in Hell (Romans 6:23). However, if we believe that Jesus our Savior died on the cross to pay the penalty for our sin we can be "saved" or born-again, our sins can be forgiven, and we enter into a personal relationship with God through Jesus Christ his son. That moment of expressing our faith in prayer is the initiation of this relationship.

Even as a five-year-old, I understood the importance of making that commitment to follow Christ. My understanding, of course, was limited by my youth but I was deeply sincere when I responded to the invitation, knelt at the altar, expressed my sorrow over sin, and pledged to follow Jesus Christ and his teachings.

Certainly, my understanding of what it meant to follow Christ was limited, yet as the years went by and I grew to understand more I renewed that pledge again and again. Thus, throughout the vast majority of my life I have recognized that God is real, that Jesus died in my place, and I have a genuine relationship with him.

This relationship has grown in its depth and quality as I have grown and matured. Although I came to faith in Christ as a child, my childish understanding of Christ has changed as I have changed over the years. In my teen years, for instance, I began to grapple with what it meant to be a Christ-follower. I made the decision in those days to put Christ first in my decisions regarding college, marriage, and occupation.

This is not to say that I have always followed Christ perfectly. I am sad to say there have been many times when I have failed to fulfill my ambition to live in obedience. I have often done or thought things that dishonor the Lord. I do not set myself up as a perfect example of what it means to follow Christ, but only as one who desires to please him in my thoughts, words, and actions.

My relationship with God has been central to my life and a key factor in coping with my disease. As a result, the Bible (which I believe to be the inspired and infallible Word of God) has been an important part of my life. I learned to study it early in life and have benefited immeasurably as a result.

Psalm 23 was one of the first passages of Scripture I memorized as a child. It has been a rich source of encouragement to me over the years. The psalm begins with the famous words, "The Lord is my shepherd . . ."

With these words David described his relationship with God as that of a sheep with the shepherd. Throughout the rest of the psalm, David illustrates God's care for his children in terms of the shepherd's care for his sheep.

He describes how the Shepherd provides him with food and drink (verses 2, 5), direction (verse 3), and protection (verse 4). Few animals are more defenseless than sheep. They have no fearsome teeth, no needle-like claws, and they don't even run fast.

Ultimately, sheep are dependent on their shepherd for survival. Thus, the good shepherd never leaves them alone in the wild. Because Jesus described himself as the Good Shepherd, (John 10:11), I can be sure he will never leave me alone. Even when I am physically by myself, I am never truly alone. I am always in his care.

I also have great confidence in the ministry of angels. In the Bible, angels are presented as heavenly beings that exist to serve God and his people. We see angels delivering messages of impending judgment (see Genesis 18, for an example). We also see them exacting God's judgment at times (Genesis 19 is one illustration). But, we are also told that angels exist to serve God's people. In fact, the book of Hebrews says it is possible to entertain angels unknowingly (Hebrews 13:2).

Therefore, we not only have the promise of his presence but the assistance of his emissaries in our times of need. I like to think of angels standing guard over my home in the times when I'm alone or walking by my side when I'm out of the house.

All of us have experienced the disappointment of a broken appointment. Someone says he or she will arrive at a particular time to perform a service or address a need, but the appointed time comes and goes and the promised visitor is nowhere to be seen. God is not so fickle as to fail to show up when promised. He has promised never to leave or forsake us.

It is easy to believe intellectually that God is with his people in every circumstance. But, it is often more difficult to believe God is with *you* in *your* circumstance. This is especially true when you recognize how far short you fall of his ideal for mankind. Satan works hard in his attempts to convince the ill that somehow God is against them, that perhaps their illness or disability is evidence that God is not on their side.

For that reason, I find Romans 8 to be a great encouragement. There Paul reminds us that our present sufferings are not comparable to the glory that awaits us (verse 18). We, and all of God's creation, groan like a woman in childbirth looking forward to the joy of a new baby. She endures the agony of labor by looking ahead to what is to come. Indeed, our bodies long for full and complete redemption, removing the scars and destruction sin has wrought. The apostle wrote, "I consider that our present sufferings are not worth comparing with the glory that will be revealed in us. (Verse 18).

While we patiently await that day, we have the promise that "in all things God works for the good of those who love him, who have been called according to his purpose (verse 28). Note that phrase, "all things." God has promised that anything he allows to enter into our lives he will use for good. That includes any illness or disability he chooses not to heal immediately. This means our physical struggles can have purpose and meaning.

Although Satan likes to tell us our struggles indicate God doesn't love us, the Bible teaches something quite different. The apostle Paul challenged the Romans with this question: ". . . if God is for us who can be against us?" (Romans 8:31b). If God has given his own Son for us, how can we deny his love for us?

"Who shall separate us from the love of God?" Paul asked. "Shall trouble or hardship or persecution or famine or nakedness or danger or sword? (Verse 35). "No, in all these things we are more than conquerors through him who loved us. For I'm convinced that neither death nor life, neither angels nor demons, neither the present nor the future, neither height nor depth, nor anything else in all creation, will be able to separate us from the love of God that is in Christ Jesus our Lord" (verses 37-39).

Not only do we have the promise of his presence and his love, believers also have promise of eternal life. When Lazarus, a friend of Jesus, became very ill his sisters, Mary and Martha, sent word to Jesus about their brother's condition. They wanted nothing more than to see Jesus come to Bethany, where they lived, and heal Lazarus as he had so many others.

Jesus, however, seemed to delay going to Lazarus until it was too late. By the time Jesus arrived, Lazarus was dead and buried in a cave-like tomb. To everyone's surprise, Jesus went to the tomb and raised Lazarus from the dead, calling him to come out as matter-of-factly as a mother calling her children for dinner.

Before doing so, Jesus made an amazing statement: "I am the resurrection and the life. The one who believes me will live, even though they die; and whoever lives by believing in me will never die. Do you believe this? (John 11:25-26). Clearly, Jesus did not mean those who believe in him would never suffer physical death, but rather that they would have eternal life in the world beyond our own.

People have asked my wife, "Is Jonathan terminal?" The answer to that question is, of course! Every one of us is terminal in the physical sense. The truth of the matter is nobody gets out alive. But, although all who follow Christ will die physically, we will live on. And we have the promise that even our physical bodies will one day be resurrected never to die again.

The psalmist, Asaph, was a man who understood this. His song, Psalm 73, makes me suspect he suffered a chronic illness or disability. We know next to nothing about him personally and my suspicion is based solely on the fact he writes like one who is familiar with such matters: "My flesh and my heart may fail, but God is the strength of my heart and my portion forever" (Psalm 73:20).

This physical body in which I now live has betrayed me to an extent. The normal, natural things I should be able to do and used to do are now beyond my capabilities. Eventually, this body will fail completely and my life on this earth will be over, but my strength is not found in my physical body but in God. I must put my trust in him. This body and indeed this earth will not remain, but he will.

We have the promise of eternal life, therefore, we do not need fear what the world can do to us. Regardless what those around us may or may not do, God has not left us to face our struggle alone.

# Chapter 11

## It's Not About Me (Or You, Either)

I believe the Bible.

I believe God created the heavens and earth and all that is in them in six days (Genesis 1).

I believe God parted the Red Sea and the people of Israel walked through on dry ground, enabling them to escape Egyptian captivity (Exodus 14).

I believe Jonah was a real man, who was called by God to preach to the city of Nineveh, and when he refused to go, God arranged for him to be swallowed by a big fish. He survived for three days in that fish's belly until the fish vomited him up on the shore (Jonah 1-4).

I believe Jesus was a real man also who was born of a virgin, performed many supernatural miracles, died on the cross, was buried in the tomb, and rose from the dead (Matthew-John).

Because I believe the Bible, I also believe God can heal the sick. Jesus healed sick people on many different occasions, sometimes in dramatic fashion. Eyes that once were blind suddenly could see. In a moment, legs that were bent and atrophied, even from birth, instantly sprang to life and the formerly lame walked away. (I always thought that was cool. Not only did a man who never walked suddenly have strength his legs, but he also learned how to walk instantly rather than the long process most people go through as toddlers!)

After Jesus had ascended back to the Father, His followers performed similar miracles. The apostles Peter and John, for instance, facilitated the healing of lame man at the temple. His illness had left him begging as his only means of survival. This man also was dramatically healed, jumping to his feet and praising God.

My belief in the biblical accounts as it relates to God's intervention in human suffering gives birth to an obvious question: Why doesn't God heal me?

This question bothered me a great deal in the early days of my illness. I would pray and pray, with no change in my condition. People prayed for me from all over the United States and many places around the world. Sometimes they would pray for me in person, even anointing me with oil, but there would be no healing. Because of today's social media, hundreds potentially thousands of people prayed for my healing. Yet, there seemed to be no answer – at least not the answer we were seeking.

So, was I missing something? Was there some prayer formula I wasn't fulfilling? Some secret words I was not using? Some gifts that I, or the people praying for me, did not possess? Was there some particular person that held the key that would open the door for healing? I looked to the Scriptures for answers.

As I studied the Bible, especially the ministry of Jesus, it seemed clear that faith had something to do with healing in numerous instances. For example, a woman was healed from years of years of incessant bleeding simply by touching the hem of Jesus' garment as he passed by. Jesus declared, "Daughter, your **faith** has made you well" (Matthew 9:22).

Jesus made similar statements to other individuals. On one occasion, Jesus told a blind man, "Go . . . your **faith** has healed you" (Mark 10:52).

When two blind men came to Jesus, in hopes of being healed, he asked them, "Do you believe that I am able to do this?" When they assured him that they did believe, Jesus said, "According to your **faith** let it be done to you." And their sight was restored (Matthew 9: 28-30).

When a blind man sitting beside the road captured the attention of Jesus, the Lord asked, "What do you want me to do for you?" The blind man replied, "Rabbi, I want to see." Jesus said, "Go, your **faith** has healed you." And the man immediately received his sight (Mark 10:46-52).

A desperate man, a synagogue leader, named Jairus, sought Jesus' help for his dying daughter. Jesus immediately went to follow the man home, but their hasty trip was interrupted by the healing of the woman with a long-standing bleeding issue. While Jesus was dealing with her, word arrived that Jairus' young daughter had died. Jesus told the young father, "Don't be afraid; just **believe**, and she will be healed" (Luke 8:50).

Even in the book of Acts, healing seems predicated by faith, particularly the faith of the one being healed. In the city of Lystra, Paul encountered a man who was lame from birth, having never walked. The man listened intently to Paul. Interestingly, the Scripture says Paul looked directly at the man, "saw that he had **faith** to be healed," and commanded him to stand to his feet. The man immediately jumped up and began to walk (Acts 14:8-10). Once again, faith seems to be the key to his healing.

The book of James, believed to be one of the earliest New Testament books, offers a faith-based prescription for dealing with illness among believers: "Is anyone among you sick? Let them call the elders of the church to pray over them and anoint them with oil in the name of the Lord. And the prayer offered in **faith** will make the sick person well; the Lord will raise them up. If they have sinned, they will be forgiven" (James 5:14-15).

So we can say, as many have, that faith is the operative factor in healing, and those who are not healed simply do not have enough faith. Question answered, problem solved . . . right?

Certainly, it is the case that many people, if not most, need to grow in faith. Whether physically sick or healthy, we all need to grow in faith.

But, while faith is, no doubt, an important part of this issue, how do we that believe the Bible explain situations in which the biblical pattern is followed and no healing takes place? Often, we blame the sufferer for having lack of faith. But is that fair? More to the point, is that biblical?

Obviously, this is a significant issue to me. Although I readily confess to weakness of faith, I have known many others of seemingly impeccable faith that have suffered long with debilitating illness and died as a result.

Not for one minute do I want to discredit the role of faith or God's ability to heal. Neither do I want to injure anyone's faith. I simply want to understand the whole of what the Bible teaches about healing.

There are, in fact, other incidents in Scripture that give us a bit of pause when it comes to assigning a lack of healing to the lack of faith.

For instance, there is the curious story of the paralyzed man brought to Jesus by four of his friends. Jesus was teaching in a house so full of people that it was impossible to take the man in the door. His friends, however, were not to be deterred so easily. They went to the roof of the house and began to disassemble the roof until they had a large hole. Using ropes tied to the four corners of the man's bed, they lowered him down into the house right in front of Jesus.

The Savior first declared that the man's sins were forgiven. The scribes and Pharisees nearby began to murmur wondering just who this man was that he could forgive sins. Knowing what they were thinking, Jesus asked if it were easier to forgive sins or to say to the paralyzed man, "Rise and walk?" Then to prove his authority to forgive sin, Jesus said to the man, "Take up your bed and go to your house." The man, being instantly healed, did exactly that.

This incident is recorded in the synoptic Gospels (Matthew, Mark, and Luke). In two of these accounts faith is mentioned, not the faith of the paralyzed man, but *the faith of his friends* (Mark 2:5; Luke 5:20). Faith, then, is still a factor, but it seems more a matter of the faith of his friends than that of the man who was healed.

In a rather odd turn of events, Jesus went to his hometown of Nazareth but was not well received. The people apparently could not think of him in terms of God's spokesman (much less God in human flesh), but only as the boy who grew up in their town. According to Matthew, Jesus did not do many miracles there because of their lack of faith (Matthew 13:58). Once again, faith is a limiting factor but it seems almost like a corporate unbelief.

This raises an interesting question: Could the lack of faith on the part of one person or group of people impact the healing of another individual? Were there people in Nazareth who could have received a miracle had there been more corporate faith? The truth is we just don't have enough information to know.

The role of faith in miraculous healing is very clear in the instances we noted. However, there are other instances in the ministry of Jesus in which no mention is made of the faith of the one who received the miracle.

Matthew tells of an instance when Jesus went into the synagogue. His constant critics, the scribes and Pharisees, were looking for an excuse to bring charges against Jesus. They found a man in the synagogue with a shriveled hand (some believe the scribes and Pharisees "planted" the man there in an attempt to trap Jesus). The Jewish religious leaders watched to see if Jesus would heal the man on the Sabbath, presuming they could charge him with violating the Law by working on the Sabbath if he were to do so.

The scribes and Pharisees asked Jesus if it was lawful to work on the Sabbath. Jesus replied, "If any of you has a sheep and it falls into a pit on the Sabbath, will you not take hold of it and lift it out? How much more valuable is a person than a sheep! Therefore, it is lawful to do good on the Sabbath" (Matthew 12:11-12).

Turning to the man, Jesus said, "Stretch out your hand." The man obeyed, and his shriveled hand was made whole. The interesting thing about this healing is that nothing is said about the man's faith. He exercised faith, of course, by stretching out his hand but no expression of faith was required as a condition of or prerequisite to his healing. In fact, Jesus decried the lack of belief among the people present.

After the death of John the Baptist, Jesus sought some time alone but was instead met by a group of people with serious needs. But when Jesus saw the large crowd, "he had compassion on them and healed their sick (Matthew 14:14). Again, no mention is made of the crowd's faith.

In Matthew 14, just after the miracle of Jesus walking on water, when the boat arrived on shore Jesus was met by a group of people seeking healing for the sick. Matthew 14:36 describes how the people asked Jesus to allow the sick to simply touch the hem of his garment, and all who did so were healed (Matthew 14:35-36). Again, there is no mention of faith on the part of those who were healed.

In Mark 1:30-31, Jesus healed Simon's mother who was sick with a fever. Nothing is said about faith either on her part or that of Simon.

Healing in the New Testament church did not always include faith as a prerequisite. Acts 28:7-8 tells of Paul healing the father of Publius, the chief official of the island Malta. Again, there is no mention of faith.

Clearly, every healing is not preceded by faith. Neither is the presence of faith a guarantee of healing. In fact, some people of faith are not healed. One possible example is found in the person of Trophimus, a believer that Paul says he left sick in the city of Miletus (2 Timothy 4:20). One wonders why Paul would leave this team member ill if healing was the usual experience of believers.

Perhaps even more insight can gained from the experience of the apostle Paul. In 2 Corinthians 12, Paul told of a man he knew that had an experience in which he was caught up into "the third heaven" (verse 2) where he heard inexpressible things, "things that no one is permitted to tell" (verse 4). At the outset of this passage one might think Paul is speaking of someone other than himself, but later it becomes clear he is referencing himself.

As a result of this experience Paul says, "Therefore, in order to keep me from becoming conceited, I was given a thorn in my flesh, a messenger of Satan, to torment me. Three times I pleaded with the Lord to take it away from me. But he said to me, "My grace is sufficient for you, for my power is made perfect in weakness" (verses 7-9).

Many, if not most, commentators view this "thorn" as some sort of physical ailment. Because of some comments the apostle made elsewhere (Galatians 4:15; 6:1) many feel that Paul's thorn in the flesh was some sort of eye problem, perhaps a lingering result of his experience on the road to Damascus that left him blind for a time (Acts 9).

Assuming this thorn in the flesh was indeed a physical ailment of some type, Paul quite clearly viewed it as satanic opposition. There is a sense in which our physical maladies have satanic origins because it was Satan who deceived Adam and Eve and unleashed death upon the human race.

Although Paul earnestly prayed, asking God to take this thorn away, the Almighty simply said his grace would be sufficient. Rather than continuing to pray for his healing, the apostle concluded, "Therefore I will boast all the more gladly about my weaknesses, so that Christ's power may rest on me" (verse 9).

Certainly, there was no lack of faith on Paul's part. Yet, the Lord refused to remove his thorn in the flesh. If this "thorn" was indeed a physical deficiency of some sort (which I believe it was), we see another instance in which God chose not to heal one of his children because he had greater things in store. He wanted to use even the messenger of Satan for the good of Paul and the church and ultimately for God's glory.

My purpose is not to denigrate the role of faith in healing, but simply to say absence of healing is not always due to a lack of faith. Death is an appointment everyone will keep; no matter who we are or how great our faith. The thing about faith-healers is that all eventually die. At least one illness or deficiency is not healed.

So what purpose could God have for allowing His child to remain ill or disabled? Why would God allow suffering to continue? Please allow me to suggest a few possibilities.

## 1. God's "No" might be a "Not yet."

Several of the people we've noted above that experienced the healing ministry of Jesus had been ill for a long time. Some had been ill since birth.

Healing was going to come, but it would be in the Father's timing as a form of authentication for the person and ministry of Jesus. Indeed, that could be the case with some believers today. It is simply not time yet in God's schedule of events for their healing to occur. Yet, it will occur in God's timing.

## 2. God might have a bigger purpose for the illness or disability.

To us, especially when we are suffering, there is often no greater good than for our suffering to be relieved. We can't imagine anything more important than to be returned to good health or to be free from our disability. But, God may have a bigger purpose than we imagine.

To the lame man that had never walked, undoubtedly nothing mattered more than his independence or being like everyone else, free to move about at will. To the blind man, God could do no greater thing than to give him sight.

To the father whose daughter was dying, there could be no bigger picture than saving his daughter's life. And, in all of these situations, the sooner it could be done the better.

God, however, had a big bigger picture in view. In light of eternity, earthly suffering is brief. In fact, as long as we live in this world, today's suffering will be followed by tomorrow's suffering. That's not meant to be pessimistic, but the reality is if the illness or disability we are fighting now doesn't kill us, something else will – eventually. Even those who were miraculously healed by Jesus had other problems later on in life that resulted in their deaths.

When we were children our parents or others in authority made decisions that we simply could not understand. Parents would say, "You're too young to stay home alone." Or, "You're too young to go to that movie." Or, "You're too young to date." We would fuss and fume and say our parents didn't understand, but many of us have the same rules for our own children because we understood that they made sense. We have come to see the bigger picture our parents saw when we were young.

God knows the end from the beginning. He knows tomorrow as well as yesterday. He knows how things work together; how one thing impacts another. This is true not only of our life but the lives of others as well, and unlike our parents, he sees all perfectly and understands it completely. It should not surprise us then that God would make decisions that we don't understand for purposes we can't see.

## 3. God's plan includes more than just us.

It is easy when you deal with an illness or disability that is there 24 hours a day, 365 days a year, to become focused only on your problem. It can absorb you and capture all your attention. This is especially true when it comes to treating a chronic illness. We run back and forth to the doctor or hospital, we often have medicine regimens around which everything else has to be planned, and our physical struggles sometimes seem to hold us, and all who love us, hostage.

Over two decades of dealing with MS has shown me that my struggles are not mine alone but impact the people around me as well, especially those who love me. I've come to believe that one reason God might have allowed me to suffer this illness is that he wanted to use my situation to accomplish good in those around me and others I can't see.

Some years ago, when I was obsessing over my condition, I prayed every day for healing. I did that with great energy and it dominated my private prayer time. One day, as I finished praying in my office, I felt the Lord speaking to me.

The last sentence might disturb you. You might wonder if I heard an audible voice, or had a great vision, or heard angels sing. None of those things occurred. I simply sensed it within.

What I sensed God saying to me was, "That's enough. I've heard your request and I will do what is best. From now on, others may pray for your healing, but you may not. I have other things for you to do."

To say the least, I was stunned. Did I just imagine this? Was this just an excuse for lack of faith? Should I share this with anyone else? These questions, and a million others, raced through my mind. I decided to keep this to myself for the time being and I did not share it with others for several years.

Once again, the Lord seemed to burn those words into my heart. My illness and my struggles were not just mine; they were intended to have an impact on those around me.

My mind went immediately to 2 Corinthians 1:3-4. The apostle Paul wrote to the Corinthians a most encouraging letter. They needed encouragement since they were suffering persecution because of their Christian faith. The apostle knew what that was like, he had suffered much persecution himself, but he encouraged the Corinthians to seek comfort in God and to share the comfort they received with others who were also suffering.

The principle was simply to share with others what God was teaching them through their time of suffering. Of course, suffering persecution and suffering an illness are two different things, but I believe the principle is still the same. God gives us comfort in our suffering so that we might share it with others who are suffering.

The suffering of the believers at Corinth, then, was not just about them. God had bigger purposes than merely easing their pain. It was not just about them living a good life or being comfortable, but rather about fulfilling the will of God and bringing glory to God in their current circumstances.

Paul didn't want them to lose sight of the big picture. Perhaps, that fledgling body of believers was suffering something similar to what I experienced. I became so focused on my disease that I was unable to consider what God might want to do through it.

One of the rigors of multiple sclerosis is that it is a 24-hour per day, 365 days a year, for the rest of your life, disease. It waxes and wanes, especially in the early years and in the relapsing remitting form of the disease. But, in the progressive form there is no relief. One goes to bed feeling the effects of the disease and wakes up to find them still there. This is true of many diseases or disabilities.

The every-day-ness of such maladies lends itself to a disease-centered, disability-focused way of thinking, the kind of thinking that results in an inward focus and often depression. Saying to yourself or to others, "I feel terrible today," over and over again does not change the fact. Nor does it leave you open to what God wants to do through you that day.

God created every person on this planet. Our Creator deserves all glory, honor, and praise. Our lives are to be lived in such a way as to magnify our God and fulfill his will on this earth. Since God knows all things past, present, and future, we can entrust our lives completely to him.

My friend, Billy Lewis, understood this well. When he was diagnosed with a particularly aggressive and hard to treat cancer, he told me, "I gave my life to Christ over 30 years ago, it is his to do with as he chooses." Billy had no death wish and he was open to healing by supernatural or medical means, but he understood that God might choose to be glorified through his disease or even his death.

God can use our trials, including our physical illnesses or disabilities, to shape us into people that are more like Christ. While a dramatic supernatural healing has its place in God's plan, our perseverance in trying times can also accomplish his purposes.

Why does God choose not to heal in some cases? It could indeed be a lack of faith, but it can also be to accomplish bigger and more wide-ranging purposes than could be fulfilled with supernatural healing. These purposes involve more than the sick individual. As James says, they will result in spiritual growth for the sufferer, but the impact is likely to be more widespread.

Personally, I've been amazed at how the Lord has used my illness to bless others. Many have spoken of how their faith has been increased by watching the Lord provide and sustain us. Others have expressed how helping us in some fashion has been a blessing to them as well as to us.

Of course, some of these people are merely on the outside looking in. They do not know the day-to-day struggle and usually see me at my best. Still, there is some measure which my suffering and God's sustaining grace in my life are an encouragement to them.

Not long ago, my wife posted a picture of me in my new power chair, praising God for this great blessing. An old friend that we haven't seen in over 30 years commented:

*I know sister it's all good and praise God for his blessing, but for me I haven't been a part for so long this is so hard for me. I love this man, he baptized me and helped me with my walk with the Lord and I just don't understand. I hope I don't upset you, but I just don't understand. Love you all and prayers to you all.*

I don't profess to know the mind of God in every situation and I understand my friend's struggle to make sense of my illness. But I find a sports analogy to be of great help.

Each year March Madness captures the attention of millions as the NCAA national basketball championship is decided with a 64-team tournament. Basketball players and coaches take center stage for a few weeks. Every team has a head coach that determines the role each player on the team will fill. Some players are starters. Some are substitutes, they come in the game to give the starters a rest or because they have a particular skill that is needed at that point in the game. The remaining players are on the team for the purpose of development (they may be starters in time) and, quite frankly, so the team has enough players to run a good practice.

Players don't always like the role they are asked to play. Bench players naturally want to be in the game, but the choice is not theirs to make. That decision belongs to the coach. In the same way, each of us has a role to play on God's "team." Unlike human coaches, our Coach fully understands each player in his or her abilities and always makes the right decision. At times, we may not like the role we are asked to play but our Coach as the big picture view. He is coaching us to the championship.

The bottom line is that it is not all about us. We are part of what God is doing in this world, and we play the role he has chosen for us. Whatever role you play, the goal is to play in such a way as to bring glory to him by encouraging others, and even challenging them. It makes life an adventure with him rather than a dreary slog through the swamp of this world. You can actually make suffering a source of joy.

James said, "Consider it pure joy, my brothers and sisters, when you face trials of many kinds, because you know that the testing of your faith produces perseverance. Let perseverance finish its work so that you may be mature and complete, not lacking anything" (James 1:2-4).

We can find comfort in knowing that our trials can make us more like Christ. But we can rejoice even more when we realize that God can use our example to help others as well. Is not just about us.

Could it be that God wants to use our illness or physical disability to help others? I think so.

# Chapter 12

## It Takes a Team

Basketball was always a source of joy and frustration in life. I played a couple of years in high school and two in college. I always thought I had the potential to play well, to be a "go-to" guy on the team, but circumstances always seemed to be against me. However, for four games at the end of my final season (my sophomore year of college) I got to live out my dream.

I played college basketball at a tiny Christian college where we struggled to even fill the team roster. This was not big time college basketball, not even close. We played schools that were like ours, and some that were bigger and better, and we lost more often than we won. However, the last four games of that season are firmly etched in my mind.

In those four games, I played like I always thought I could. In the last game of our regular season I scored 24 points and grabbed 19 rebounds. The next three games were in our league tournament and I averaged 19 points and 10 rebounds per game. I felt like a star.

The only problem was, we won only two of those games. It was great for me that I had four good games, but victory requires more than one player doing well. In fact, as every coach knows, it is even possible for the "good game" of one player to hurt the team's chances to win.

One thing I've learned in the course of dealing with my MS is that a chronic illness is not a single-person experience. To successfully navigate the ups and downs of any disease or disability requires a team, a group of people committed to the same cause. This team includes family, friends, medical professionals, caregivers, and hopefully, a loving and supportive church family.

**Family**

I have been blessed, first and foremost, with a loving and supportive wife. Shortly after my diagnosis I read that the divorce rate among MS patients was 60%. That's been a number of years ago and the figure may not be accurate today, at least I hope not. But it does highlight the fact that chronic disease is not just the concern of the patient. When one has a disease or disability it has a life-changing effect on everyone who is close to them.

Dianna and I have been married for over four decades. We've have had a deeply satisfying and rich relationship over those four decades. She's my best friend, the person I most like to spend time with. But we are not the same people we were when we married in 1977. We are, of course, older and hopefully wiser. We've weathered the ups and downs of parenting, financial difficulties, grief, occupational success and failure, relocation, change of careers, etc. But, nothing has been as hard as dealing with the changes and challenges MS has brought into our lives in recent years.

For many years while our children were home, we made a point of going out to dinner once a month, just the two of us, and taking overnight getaways three or four times a year. However, those special times as a couple are much more difficult these days. The reality is that my condition requires a lot of attention and Dianna is often more of a caregiver and I am more of a patient than we are romantic partners.

It's hard to get excited about going to dinner when there are so many obstacles. She has to get me cleaned up and dressed, place me into my power chair so she can dress, put me into the car (not an easy task by any means), load whatever chair or equipment I need, drive to wherever we are going, get me out of the car and inside the restaurant, and help me get situated.

Once we get settled at the table she often has to read the dinner options to me (depending on how my double vision is doing that day and how the menu is printed), request any special accommodations (such as a cup with a lid and straw since I have a tendency to knock things over) and often make sure the food is in small bites so as not to cause me to choke.

In addition, she has to prepare and bring my meds and because of my swallowing issues keep an eye on me to be sure I'm not getting too tired or being careless about the way I eat (bites that are too large, eating too fast, not swallowing correctly, etc.). Several times she has had to come around the table to slap me on the back and dislodge a bite that wouldn't go down.

When the meal is over, she has to get me back in the car, drive home, get me out of the car and into the house, help me get undressed, take me to the toilet, and take care of about a million other details. And, that's just to go to dinner. The list is infinitely longer when it comes to out-of-town overnight travel.

The tasks most couples share fall to her. She pays the bills (my double vision makes it impossible for me), she does the banking, she washes the car, she changes lightbulbs, she checks out strange noises in the night, she files income taxes, she answers the mail, takes the car for service, lifts the heavy stuff, does all the driving (we have agreed that though I still have a license, driving is not a good idea for me . . . or the other people on the road), makes minor repairs around the house, etc. It is no wonder that she is tired!

In a tense moment, when I was frustrated about the way she was doing something, I said, "*I'm* the one with the disease," implying that she should do it my way. "I realize that," she replied, "but you are not the only one; I have MS, too!" She's right. While I may be the one with the disease, she also has to deal with the ramifications.

It would be wonderful if I could report that we never have a conflict or difference of opinion, but that wouldn't be true. Occasionally, she makes a decision I don't like. From time to time I have expectations that are unrealistic. We can't avoid butting heads every now and then, but for any marriage to work, couples have to give and take. This is never truer than when one has a serious illness or disability.

To make matters worse, about 3% of MS patients suffer a degree of dementia. While a very small percentage can actually be said to have dementia, many chronically ill people suffer from what I would call "distortia." Chronic illness and disability, and the accompanying loss of control and security, have a way of distorting things that are said and done.

Fears like being put into a rest home, the well spouse being unfaithful, being a burden to others, and even being taken advantage of can be blown up to ridiculous extremes with little or no provocation. Dealing with this kind of problem requires tremendous self-discipline on the part of one who is ill and the spouse.

Dianna is fond of saying with a smile that she has never considered divorce in our 40 years of marriage, but she has on occasion given some thought to murder. (A sentiment she got from Ruth Graham, the wife of Billy Graham.)

We have often turned to 1 Corinthians 13:4-8 to re-calibrate our attitudes. The Apostle Paul wrote, "Love is patient, love is kind. It does not envy, it does not boast, it is not proud. It does not dishonor others, is not self-seeking, and is not easily angered, it keeps no record of wrongs. Love does not delight in evil but rejoices with the truth. It always protects, always trusts, always hopes, and always perseveres. Love never fails."

Over the years, a number of people (especially newly-weds or singles hoping to marry) have told us they would like to have a marriage like ours. Our response is usually something like, "You can, but it takes a lot of work."

Building and maintaining a strong marriage requires a lot of self-restraint. It means saying no to what one wants in order to do what is best for the other. It means being patient, kind, humble, seeking what is best for the other person, biting your tongue, trusting, and persevering.

A number of years ago when my son was in college he asked me how a person could know the right person to marry. I told him the same thing I've told many people as a pastor. Based on what 1 Corinthians 13 says about love, I think you are ready for marriage only when what is best for the other individual is more important to you than pleasing yourself or even doing what is best for you.

In other words, until you can say that the well-being and best interests of the other person are so important to you that you would step aside if it were not in their best interest to marry you, you are not ready to marry. I know that's a high standard but it means that I must be willing right from the start to put the other person first and to do what is best for him or her even if it's not comfortable for me. That's what makes a marriage work.

The involvement of children in the care of a chronically ill or disabled parent depends, of course, on their age. While children need to understand the limitations of the ill parent and assist where it is reasonable, young children should not be made to bear the burden of the situation. It is reasonable to require children to help, but it is not reasonable to expect their lives to revolve around their parent's misfortune.

I do believe, however, that grown children bear some responsibility when it comes to caring for their aging, disabled, or ill parents. Although they live some distance away, our children have been faithful to that responsibility.

## Doctors

Physicians are also vital members of the team. The chronically ill person will probably have more than one physician. I have a neurologist that specializes in multiple sclerosis, a primary care physician for matters such as high blood pressure, and an ophthalmologist (eye specialist) that I see on a regular basis. In addition, I have seen a host of other specialists for the varied symptoms that go with MS.

These days, almost all of my doctors are connected to Vanderbilt University, one of the leading medical groups, educational institutions, and hospitals in the South. But, even before I moved to Tennessee I saw one of the leading multiple sclerosis specialists on the West Coast. Quality medical care is essential. Get the best available in your area.

## Caregivers

Whether or not the chronically ill or disabled person is married, there is often a need for a caregiver. In the early stages, this may be a spouse or even a friend, especially if the ill person is not severely disabled. When the physical or mental deficiencies grow serious enough that the patient is not safe when left alone, professional caregiving often becomes necessary.

Even after my significant downturn in the summer of 2015 had left me unable to work, I tried to stay at home alone while Dianna was at work. But numerous falls and subsequent calls to the fire department to come pick me up out of the floor, not to mention the injuries, made clear my need for more assistance. On the recommendation of friends we hired a professional caregiver to be with me while Dianna was at work.

This team member, actually several from the same firm that rotate days, has been an untold help. Having a caregiver has eased my mind in that I'm not left to fend for myself. My caregiver fixes breakfast and lunch, helps me to the restroom, picks up the countless things I drop, and assists me in a variety of other ways. This also sets Dianna's mind at ease because she doesn't worry that I will fall or injure myself in some manner by trying to do for myself.

It is, of course, not a cheap solution. My caregiver has worked with us financially to help us make ends meet and many friends have contributed financially to help ease the burden. This is something I did without for a long time, but I have seen the importance of having a caregiver on my team.

It is important that this decision not be made carelessly. There are many families that can testify of abuse, theft, and neglect at the hand of an unqualified caregiver. This choice is probably best made on the recommendation of good friends with personal experience with the caregiver.

## Church Family

In my opinion, the team is not complete without a loving church family. As Christians, Dianna and I feel church attendance and participation is important. We are part of the body of Christ, the invisible union of believers with Jesus and one another. The local church is a visible expression of that invisible body.

Just as every physical body is not healthy, some churches are unhealthy. Some churches are full of self-centered people who are not interested in serving others. They ignore needs in their fellowship and their community. This is not what Christ desires his church to be all about. If that sounds like your experience with church, I'm sorry. It is probably time to seek a healthier fellowship. I urge you not to give up on the people of God as a whole.

Since moving to Nashville, we have been members of The Donelson Fellowship. This church has a long history of good spiritual health. Nevertheless, merely attending worship services with approximately 1000 other church parishioners would not have resulted in the kind of care we've experienced. While the pastoral staff members are friends, and always available to us, our involvement in a small group within the church has made all the difference.

We are part of a Life Group called, The Barnabas Project. This group consists of people who are at a similar stage of life for the most part, although we have some younger singles and couples in our group. We are called a Life Group because we are "doing life together." These individuals have been "Jesus with skin on" to us in a myriad of ways. When I have been hospitalized they have cared for Dianna with meals, home maintenance, encouragement, and occasional financial support. When I have been home they continue to show this kind of support and love on us.

While we have struggled to afford the level of caregiving I need (and no, our insurance will not pay for it), they have stepped up as individuals and as a group to help us financially. Members of the group have provided our lawn care, paid our expenses for group retreat, provided home repairs, paid for the repair of my lift recliner, made it possible for us to visit relatives and contributed to expenses we incur when relatives visit us.

The group as a whole purchased a high-end walker for me, one that was suitable for my taller-than-average height and much more serviceable than what was provided by the insurance company. Members of the group paid for my first power chair, built (and provided all the material for) a ramp at our home, do ongoing lawn maintenance, and much more. These are only a few of the practical provisions this group has made for us.

More important, they have been there to encourage us and support us in prayer on a daily basis. Nothing means more to me than that kind of love and care. We moved to Nashville so I could take a position as an editor with Randall House Publications. This move put us at some physical distance from our children, grandchildren, and parents. Our brothers and sisters in Christ have stepped in to fill the gaps.

This "team" approach to life may be unusual in our day, but it is consistent with the biblical pattern for life in the body of Christ. We are not the only recipients of the love and kindness of our Life Group. Others have experienced practical support when facing illness, grief, court appearances, divorce, etc.

I have learned that God doesn't intend for any of us to go through life alone. We need the support of others. It took the loss of my physical independence and abilities to recognize that fact.

# Chapter 13

# God Provides

By Saturday night I had all I could take. The pain in my gut had been getting worse since early in the day. Finally, I concluded that going to the ER was my only choice.

It was the summer of 1977. Dianna and I had been married only a few weeks. It was our first medical crisis as a couple.

At the emergency room, they took x-rays, poked and prodded, and asked lots of questions. Eventually, they gave me some pain meds and sent me home. Their conclusion was a rather indefinite finding of a "spastic colon."

The worst part was not the exam or the x-rays or even the vague diagnosis. The worst part by far was when they asked for payment. With no medical insurance, I was expected to pay in full on the spot. Thankfully, we both got paid on Friday so I had the money to pay the bill. The only problem was that there was nothing left. Our bills were up-to-date and our cars were full of gas but we had not bought groceries. In those days, we needed only $20 to buy groceries for a week.

I still wasn't feeling well by morning, so Dianna went on to church alone while I slept in.

Dianna sang in the choir so she left her purse in the pew where she planned to sit after the choir was dismissed. We weren't together physically, but psychologically we were on the same page. Both of us were fretting about how we would buy groceries for the week.

We had made a commitment to God and each other to give a tithe (10 percent) of our income to the Lord through his church. That paycheck our tithe amounted to $20, the amount we needed for groceries. Just before leaving for church, Dianna asked if she should pay our tithes. In a moment of faith I answered, "Yes!" But, my faith didn't last long.

As soon as she left, I began to panic. *What are we going to do? What was I thinking? Can I call the church in time to stop her?* (Remember, no cell phones in 1977!) *What would she think of me, anyway?*

After church, when Dianna came through the door of our tiny apartment I was immersed in a cloud of gloom. I had prayed, to be sure, but mostly I had worried, seeing no solution to our dilemma. However, my bride was beaming and nearly bursting to tell me why.

"I went to the choir like usual, and left my purse sitting in the pew," she said. "I prayed that somehow God would provide what we needed. Then when I went to the car to go home, I opened my purse to get the car keys and found this inside, lying on top."

It took me a minute to realize what she was waving at me. It was a $20 bill. I was speechless. "Don't you see, God answered our prayers? We can buy groceries!" she triumphantly proclaimed.

I was stunned. Did God simply create a $20 bill in Dianna's purse? I had no doubt he could do it, but it seemed unlikely that he would choose to do so.

I concluded instead that God had moved on someone's heart to give us $20 anonymously by slipping it into Dianna's purse while she was in the choir. I was even more amazed. Did the person who gave that money know about our trip to the hospital? Did he or she understand our plight? Why did this person want to be anonymous?

There was no one to thank, but God. Maybe that's the way he wanted it. He didn't desire to create in us a great faith in humanity or confidence in our fellow man. He did desire to deepen our faith in him and increase our confidence that he could provide for our needs.

Right at the outset of our marriage, God wanted to instill in us that he could be trusted. It was only the first of many times when God would provide for us in unexpected ways.

The Bible says, "And my God will meet all your needs according to the riches of his glory in Christ Jesus" (Philippians 4:19). This is God's promise to all his children. This is the essence of Psalm 23:1, because Lord is my shepherd "I lack nothing." The King James Version says, "I shall not want."

This is a huge promise. Because God is my shepherd and I am his sheep I need not fear that I will lack anything I need. Now be careful not to use this as an excuse for being lazy. God expects us to work if we are able. As my grandfather, Joseph E. Yandell said, "If you can work and make big money, then work and make big money. If you can only work and make a little money, then work and make little money. If you can work and make no money, then work anyway; because work is good for the mind."

We also need to read the verse carefully. God does not promise to meet all "our greed's." He is not giving us a blank check for whatever toy or trip or bobble we desire. The promise is that he will supply our needs in proportion to the riches of the glory of Christ. Since there is no end to his riches of glory, there is no need that he cannot supply.

Dianna and I have found this to be true in countless ways throughout our 40 years of marriage. It began with the mysterious appearance of the $20 bill and has continued throughout the ensuing years.

That provision has taken many forms. Sometimes it has been in the form of anonymous gifts. Other times, it has simply been in the form of additional work (more hours resulting in more pay, part-time jobs, unexpected tax returns, etc.). In some instances, it has taken the more humbling form of face-to-face gifts from other people.

That $20 gift was the beginning of a lifelong chain of God's blessings extended to us by the hand of his people. I can't begin to list all we have received, but I'll try to remember some highlights of God's blessings over the years.

Early in our marriage, things were tough. After a few months of high rent living ($155 per month, all bills paid) in Moore, Oklahoma, a suburb on the south side of Oklahoma City, we moved into the City to a duplex that rented for $65 a month (no bills paid). Unfortunately, it had no stove, no air-conditioning, and poor heating. When it snowed, a mound of snow piled up by the front door on the patchwork "carpeting" that consisted of various shapes and sizes of carpet (none larger than one square foot) taped toAA the hardwood floor like a collage.

With no stove, we ate a lot of potted meat, peanut butter and jelly, and whatever we could find that didn't require cooking. On rare occasions, we would go for a burger at the drive-in but it was always served with guilt because we knew we couldn't really afford it. Even in those days the Lord took care of us. As college students, as long as school was in session we were able to eat some meals on campus. We cut corners everywhere else and managed to make ends meet.

**FROM JONATHAN'S JOURNAL**: *10/6/10 "To borrow a phrase I heard today, ' My Father gives nothing but good gifts.' I confess that I do not see well in some of my present circumstances, but by faith I will believe Your Word and act accordingly as you provide grace."*

When we moved to California after my sophomore year, my first item of business was finding a job. I anticipated a long struggle. But, as God would have it, my brother-in-law, Dan Steigman, worked in the office at Sandpointe, a mobile home plant owned by the Fleetwood Corporation. At his suggestion, I filled out an application to work on the production line. Then, after I left, Dan dug it out of the pile of applications, placed it on top, and told a foreman that I would make a good employee. I was hired a day or two later. For the next three and half years that job helped put food on the table while I continued schooling at California Christian College in Fresno.

In the fall of 1980, I began preaching on a weekly basis at a small church in Tulare, California. I continued to do so until early 1981 when we received word that Sandpointe was closing. I was faced with a dilemma, do I look for another job, accept the offer of a job with Fleetwood in Stockton, California, or seek some other opportunity?

Things had been bad at the plant for some time. We worked 2 to 3 days a week because orders were few. I made ends meet by doing yardwork, using my dad's tools. Just when it looked like we would not have enough money to cover our bills I would get more yard work. I didn't really enjoy working at Sandpointe but every attempt to find a different job was a dead end.

When I told the board at the church about the situation, they offered me a full-time position as pastor including a salary and a parsonage to live in. Although the position was "full-time" the salary was not quite sufficient. Once again, the Lord provided yardwork to help us get by. We never missed a meal.

In fact, an older couple in the church, Eulis and Verna Bradshaw, made a point of taking us out for Sunday lunch at places we could never afford. He was a retired service station owner and provided us with a variety of work on our car. Coupled with the mechanical acumen of an old friend, Phil Wood (who also served as the music director of our church), they kept our car in good shape.

The Lord's goodness to us continued when we moved to Sacramento to start a new church. As noted in part 1, the goal of a new church was never achieved. However, we continued to pray, trust God, and watch him meet our needs.

One of the chief means by which this was accomplished was the beginning of my work with Randall House Publications. It began with a phone call from Dr. Jonathan Thigpen, the editor of the Sunday school curriculum for adults. He asked me to write a portion of the teaching guide for the weekly Bible study curriculum. After some assignments from him, I was asked to do other things. As time went on I was invited to do more writing focusing on teens rather than adults.

This writing was time-consuming and certainly wouldn't make one rich, but it helped us financially. It came at a time when we were struggling to pay our bills. I considered it God's provision for our needs and rejoiced that I could do something I enjoy doing to help make ends meet.

Writing Bible study curriculum for Randall House supplemented our income for years to come, even when I accepted the pastorate of a church in Garden Grove, California. The move resulted in a little more salary due to the fact that the church had a parsonage.

God's provision surprised me yet again the first time I needed a primary care doctor after moving to Garden Grove. When I asked around for recommendations the director of the church's preschool strongly suggested I see her doctor. I took her recommendation and made an appointment. I found the staff extremely cordial and the doctor very helpful. When I went to pay, I took out my checkbook and prepared to write a check when the woman at the desk said, "I'm sorry, your money doesn't spend here."

After a few minutes of confusion, she finally made me understand that the doctor gave pastors free medical care. It was the beginning of several years of free care adding up to many thousands of dollars. The doctor would accept whatever the insurance would pay no matter the amount. This courtesy extended to Dianna and the kids as well. It was a gift that made a powerful impact on our budget and health for years to come.

In my experience, God's provision for our financial needs most often has been in the form of additional work. Some people seem to be allergic to work. It causes them to break out in a rash or a sneezing fit, I suppose. Whatever it is, such people would never consider taking on another job or creating a business on the side. They would rather complain about God not meeting their needs.

I am thankful that my father taught me the value of work and that no work is "beneath" me, no one owes me anything. When I was young, some people told me they wouldn't wash dishes, bus tables, cut grass, or pull weeds for a living. Dad taught by his words and example that work was honorable. It is better to be underpaid or undervalued than to be unemployed when there is work to be found.

Those involved in ministry are not exempt. While churches should never expect a pastor to take employment on the side, it is far better for a pastor to do what is necessary to provide for his family than it is to complain about the church and his salary. Dad proved this principle when I was young by working two-side jobs (driving a school bus and door-to-door sales) while pastoring a church.

Work is a blessing, not a curse. Some associate work with being part of the curse against mankind as a result of sin, but in fact Adam had a "job" even before he did anything wrong. Genesis 2:11 says God put man in the Garden of Eden "to work it and take care of it." It was only after Adam and Eve's sin that God cursed the ground, making Adam's work laborious and wearisome.

So, although I wanted to write other things, when I was asked to write Bible study materials I considered it to be God's provision for our needs, just as I had when I mowed lawns to supplement my pastoral income in my first church.

God's provision was also seen in more subtle ways. For a 12-year period we took our vacation at Pismo Beach on the central coast of California near San Luis Obispo. We liked the small town feel, the sense of safety, and the close proximity of things we enjoyed. We often vacationed there with my parents. Dad and I particularly enjoyed fishing nearby Santa Margarita Lake.

Richard W. Lindberg, a retired aerospace engineer and one of the men in the Garden Grove church, also enjoyed that area of the state. In fact, the license plate frame on his car said, "I love the SLO life." (SLO referred to San Luis Obispo County.)

McClintock's was perhaps the most famous restaurant in Pismo Beach. The steaks there were almost legendary. Rich knew the cost of the restaurant was beyond what our vacation budget could handle, so he made a point of giving me a $100 bill before we left on vacation each year with the instruction, "Take your family to McClintock's." Each year on vacation we enjoyed a steak dinner that was beyond our means because of this brother's kindness. I considered this to be another expression of God's provision, albeit not for a "need."

There were, of course, many of such kindnesses we enjoyed: tickets to Disneyland, annual passes to Knott's Berry Farm, countless dinners out, numerous small gifts. Twice we received the gift of accommodations in Palm Springs — once it came from a church member that won them at work and another time as a gift from ministry friends. These were also the provision of God.

Nothing compares to the way in which we have seen God's provision in recent years.

Our daughter's two boys were born with health challenges, likely due to the fact that both boys were born a few weeks premature.

**FROM JONATHAN'S JOURNAL**: *10/14/10*

*My Hiding Place, You have been a shelter for me on countless occasions. Last night's entry was interrupted by yet another blessing from Your hand! . . . A sister from church called to offer her frequent flyer miles to us so Dianna can go to OKC to see Cassie and family during next week's fall break. It is an answer to prayer and a wonderful gift!"*

During the time when both boys were in precarious health circumstances, we often requested prayer for them in church. A woman we hardly knew came to Dianna and explained that she had frequent flyer miles that she wasn't going to use and were soon to expire. She offered to give those miles to Dianna so she could fly to Oklahoma City to be with our daughter and the grand-sons. Dianna, of course, gratefully accepted her offer.

A few months later, we opened the back door at our house to discover that the back deck was about 12 to 18 inches lower than it used to be and tilted precariously. We soon discovered the deck had pulled away from the house and was collapsing. We sought advice from friends, but no one had a solution we could afford.

It was still unrepaired when time came for our vacation. Since our vacation involved other family members, just skipping it was not an option. We prayed about the situation for several days and decided we would just deal with it after vacation, a trip to Dianna's parents' home on Grand Lake in Oklahoma. We had planned to begin the 10 to 12-hour drive early in the morning, shortly after dawn. Much to our frustration, our departure was later previously than we had previously planned.

As we were loading the car we noticed unexpected cars pulling up out front. We asked the first couple that arrived what they were doing. Rather sheepishly they explained that they thought we would be gone already and a group of people from the church were gathering to begin work on our deck. "By the time you get home," they said, "You will have an entirely new deck." They intended it as a surprise but our late departure spoiled it.

**FROM JONATHAN'S JOURNAL:** 7/19/11

*'I continue to rejoice at Your amazing provision for the replacement of our deck. Our brothers and sisters in the Lord provided all the material and labor. It is and a great addition to the house. And it all happened in a way I could never have imagined. I am both humbled and amazed."*

True to their word, we returned home to discover a brand-new deck. It was completely finished and there was no cost to us for labor or material!

We considered it nothing less than an answer to prayer. God had provided in a most unexpected manner. We gave him praise.

Sometime later, I was asked to teach The Barnabas Project life group while their usual teacher was working on his Master's degree. I readily agreed and thoroughly enjoyed teaching this group made up largely of spiritually mature believers. It was while I was teaching this group that I endured my most serious hospitalization. Due to the advance of my multiple sclerosis and a few complicating factors, I spent eight days in the hospital, came home for five days, went back to the hospital, and eventually to rehab for two weeks.

During that time our son, our daughter, my sister, and my parents all came to Nashville, staying at our home. The Barnabas Project stepped-up amazingly. They gave food, cash, gift cards, and countless kindnesses to make the situation better.

In the nearly two years since that hospitalization these dear brothers and sisters in Christ have given and given and given even more. They purchased a custom-made walker for me, built a wheelchair ramp on our front porch, provided us with meals repeatedly, mowed our grass, given us countless gift cards, and provided thousands of dollars to assist in paying for caregivers.

Just as I was completing this section, we found ourselves in another tough spot. Caregiving is expensive. Even though my caregivers are giving us a discount, 35 hours of care per week ads up to a lot of money. Although our insurance has been generous in covering a lot of expenses, caregiving is not among them. The cost was beyond our budget and we had to dip into our meager savings regularly to cover it.

As we watched our savings dwindle we knew we could not continue like this. Again and again, we prayed asking God to meet our need. Different people, family and friends alike, had told us to call on them if we ever need anything. Still, we chose not to make our need known to anyone but God.

We did, however, make a change in the caregiving schedule, reducing it to only 30 hours per week. I felt I could get by with fewer hours of assistance as the situation demanded it.

The following week, we went to Life Group and church on Sunday as usual. As a friend casually shook hands with Dianna he slipped her a wad of bills. She discreetly accepted them with a puzzled look on her face. He said simply, "Somebody gave me these to give to you. They wanted to remain anonymous and don't ask who it was because I don't even remember."

Dianna was stunned. As our friend walked away she glanced down at the bills in her hand and dropped them into her purse. Later, as we took the elevator down to the worship center she whispered to me, "Those were $100 bills." On the way home from church I counted 20 of them — $2000. Enough to pay for over six week's caregiving! Once again, God answered our prayers!

This list is certainly incomplete, but I don't know how we could possibly total up the value of gifts we have received.

One thing you'll notice is that none of these provisions of God were miraculous in the sense that they were created from the dust or molded out of thin air. Each one passed through human hands, provided by people motivated to act by the Spirit of God.

I don't mean to imply that God is incapable of miraculous provision. The Bible records instances in which God seems to create food or resources out of nothing. The most famous such incident is when God provided Manna for Israel to eat in the wilderness (Exodus 16).

We should also recognize the gifts of others as one means of God's provision for us. We may be humbled by such gifts, but we should not refuse them or allow ourselves to feel like freeloaders.

Additionally, it should cause us to take seriously the prompting we feel to give to others. We should be open to the way the Lord wants to use us. If he prompts us to give to others in need we should obey and thank God for the opportunity. I'm convinced that God wants to use believers to meet each other's needs. That doesn't mean our assets must go into one pool. But it does mean that our assets belong to God and we should use them as he directs.

We must never forget that everything we own is a gift. Ultimately, it all comes from the hand of our Creator. Therefore, we are obligated to learn to use it, gain it, and give it in a way that pleases him. God may provide for us through employment or additional work or even the gifts of others. But, in the end, the provision comes from him regardless of the form it takes. We can depend upon him to meet our needs, whatever they may

# Chapter 14

## Expect and Embrace Opposition

James said, "Consider it pure joy, my brothers and sisters, whenever you face trials of many kinds, because you know that the testing of your faith produces perseverance. Let perseverance finish its work so that you may be mature and complete, not lacking anything" (James 1:2-4).

James was writing originally to believers undergoing great persecution. His original audience was largely Jewish people that had come to faith in Christ. They suffered intense persecution from their fellow Jews who felt the Hebrew Christians had betrayed their heritage and the Law. This persecution might include simply refusing to do business with them and ostracizing them within the Jewish community, but could go as far as arrest, trial, and even execution.

James viewed whatever level of persecution they were encountering as being a test of their faith. The Greek word translated as "testing" is a word that referred to proving or ascertaining the genuineness or purity of something. James saw the various trials they were encountering as an opportunity to prove or demonstrate the genuineness of their faith in Christ.

The apostle therefore urged his readers to see these trials as cause for joy. It is through these trials, James argued, that they would learn perseverance and their faith would grow and mature, becoming more whole and complete.

Like most evangelical Christians, I believe these words to be inspired by the Holy Spirit, intended for the edification or building up of believers in all generations from the time of the writing until now and even beyond. While most of us have not endured the type of persecution experienced by the first readers of the epistle of James, we do experience "various kinds of trials." Chronic illness, disability, or infirmity of any type could certainly qualify as such a testing or trial.

In my mind, one thing is for sure: Chronic illness will test your faith. In my experience, this testing may take a variety of forms: jealousy, fear, battle fatigue, relationship challenges, doubt, discouragement, and idleness. Please allow me to address each of these briefly.

**Jealousy or envy** is something few people want to admit. Maybe that's because we secretly hear mother's voice telling us we shouldn't feel that way. Mom was right, of course, but that doesn't solve our problem, does it? It is hard not to be jealous or envious when we see others, especially the ungodly, prospering physically and materially while we do not. I find it frustrating to see people using their physical strength to do evil.

If you can relate to my struggle, be assured we are not alone. Asaph, the author of Psalm 73, expressed a similar sentiment when he confessed to almost slipping, losing his spiritual foothold, because he was envious of the wicked (Psalm 73:1-4). The psalmist described his frustration with the fact that the wicked seem to prosper with impunity. The absence of judgment, in the eyes of the psalmist, had led the proud to doubt God's existence (verses 5-12). This state of affairs leaves the psalmist feeling like he has cleansed his heart in vain because, while the wicked are doing well, he feels as though he's been plagued (verses 14-16).

I can't help but wonder if Asaph suffered from a chronic illness or disability. There is not a lot to go on other than the word "plagued" in verse 14 and the general tone of Psalm 73 as a whole. Yet, whether or not Asaph suffered from a chronic illness or disability, his struggle to understand why the wicked prospered while he suffered is a familiar one to those of us who battle chronic illness.

Personally, I have never been close to abandoning my faith or giving up on God. I have, however, found myself questioning what I know about God based on Scripture. For instance, the Bible clearly states that God is compassionate, merciful, and just. (God himself said so in Exodus 34:6-7.) But when I look at what some believers, people of genuine faith, have to deal with I have, on occasion, been puzzled.

I see godly men and women living on a pittance, struggling to keep food on the table, while the wicked live in lavish excess. I see godly men who have devoted their lives to the ministry die young of savage diseases while wicked men seemingly live long and healthy lives. I see men and women that live in careless sexual promiscuity bring children into this world that they don't even want while godly couples that maintain sexual integrity are childless.

These and many more seeming incongruities can cause us to question God's Word or his character. If God is so good, why am I so miserable? If God is merciful, why does my suffering continue? If God gives grace to those who need it, why am I at the end of my rope?

The problem is that we get confused about God's purposes. His goal is not to make us happy but to make us holy. His purpose is not to make us comfortable but make us Christ-like. Our job is not to understand or critique his actions but to persevere through whatever trials we may face to accomplish his purposes.

James could make an audacious statement like, "Consider it pure joy, my brothers and sisters, whenever you face trials of many kinds" because he was challenging readers to look beyond the momentary discomfort to see the ultimate benefits. There is, in fact, no logical reason to consider our trials a cause for joy other than the one suggested by James. We can find joy in our trials only when we see beyond them to what God is accomplishing in and through us.

But, how does one get to that place? Asaph said the whole issue was troublesome to him until he entered the sanctuary of God (Psalm 73:16-17). It was in worship that Asaph came to realize that the wicked are on slippery ground, that in the end they will be completely swept away (verses 18-19). The whole thing brought the psalmist to repentance over his attitude (verses 21-24).

I've been there. Perhaps you have, too.

**Fear** is another factor that tests our faith. Chronic illness can make us fearful for our safety and the safety of those we love.

I remember a discussion in a men's group made up of MS patients. There was a debate among the men about whether it was best to get a handicap license plate or to merely use a handicap placard when using handicap parking. One man said he would never have a handicap license plate because he felt like it made him a target for thieves and robbers. His illness had made him fearful.

Chronic illness can also cause one to be fearful of the future. I have known of several individuals who have taken their own lives rather than face the likelihood of the severe disability.

**FROM JONATHAN'S JOURNAL:**
*12/3/10*

*"I have no need to fear, for man can do nothing to me. Ultimately, even if my physical life were snuffed out I would be unharmed. Nothing done to my flesh, be it by man or disease, can separate me from You."*

I confess, I have been guilty of both of these types of fear. When I was healthy, I felt I could physically defend myself or my family in the case of attack. Prior to the downturn in my health, I was sure I would remain ambulatory and relatively strong for the rest of my life. Now the reality of my weakness in the progression of disease tends to open the door to fear.

In those moments when fear threatens to overwhelm us we must put our confidence in the One that said, "I will be with you always." When we are fearful we must put our trust in him, knowing that he will not abandon us no matter what we suffer.

God does not intend his children to be shackled by fear. As Paul wrote, "For the Spirit God gave us does not make us timid, but gives us power, love and self-discipline" (2 Timothy 1:7). We can say with David, "When I am afraid, I put my trust in you" (Psalm 56:3).

**Battle fatigue** is how I describe weariness. The Christian life is an upstream battle. We swim against the flow of our world. When you add chronic illness or a disability to that mix it is easy to become weary in the fight. Soldiers that suffer from battle fatigue are of limited value to their unit. They may be present and going through the motions, but they may be more hindrance than help.

I have found that the key to beating battle fatigue is proper rest and good nutrition. Every soldier needs a break now and then. And soldiers suffering from malnutrition make poor combatants.

Prior to my disability, I always had so many irons in the fire I couldn't possibly keep up. I also found it hard to slow down enough to worship. While rest and good nutrition are important in the physical realm, I've come to realize worship provides the rest I need to function well.

As a pastor, I rarely entered into worship myself. I was too busy making sure everything went right so others could worship. When I stepped out of the pastorate I took on other responsibilities that kept me distracted. Now I'm learning, and I emphasize *learning*, to worship.

I also have a new appreciation for personal devotion or what some call quiet time. I used to always be focused on a message or a lesson or something else I was planning to teach. My personal devotional time became just another venue of study.

One problem that has contributed greatly to my disability is double vision. My doctors agree that the nerves in my brain simply cannot coordinate the images from each eye. As a result, reading is difficult and when I'm tired it's almost impossible. This makes reading Scripture difficult, to say the least.

**FROM JONATHAN'S JOURNAL:** *4/12/96 "Dianna has been having a tough time with it all lately. She has been so supportive, so compassionate, and so loving, every step of the way. I know she'll be there for me if she's capable – come what may. She's suffered staggering losses due to this stuff. Her life has radically changed."*

I have learned instead to listen to the Scripture being read, either by Dianna or through You Version on my phone. This has given me a new way to get the spiritual nutrition I need to continue the battle. No soldier in God's army can survive without the rest that comes through worship or the nourishment that is found in Scripture and prayer.

**Relationship challenges**, I must admit, caught me by surprise. I never imagined the difficulties a serious disability could bring into relationships of every type. It is most difficult, of course, on those who are closest to me.

Dianna and I have been married 40 years. We've been through numerous financial challenges, the rearing of two children, the difficulties of 20+ years in the pastorate, moving across the country from our children, and career changes. Both of us agree, however, that nothing has been more challenging then my MS and subsequent disability.

Because of my disability, Dianna's workload has changed tremendously. (I think that is true of all spouses of the disabled.) My disability has left me unable do maintenance around the house, mow the yard, pay bills, run errands, drive a car, and countless other tasks. Circumstances have forced her into taking on those responsibilities as well as caring for me (a difficult task by itself).

The days of spontaneous activity are gone. Just taking me to church is a major difficulty fraught with possibilities of disaster. We have ended a simple trip to the mall with me lying in the parking lot beside the car and her asking strangers to help me into the vehicle. Every time she walks in the door at home she is confronted with someone who needs her help and may have a mess to clean up.

We've always had the kind of marriage that others aspire to. While it has required work it has been a joyful challenge. My disability has made it exceedingly more difficult.

Somewhere down the road I'm sure we will be able to share with others the secrets of maintaining a strong marriage in the midst of disability, but at the moment we are holding on for dear life. We are knit together by love for Christ, love for one another, and a commitment we made on June 30, 1977 to love, honor, and cherish one another until death parts us.

Watching my decline has been unbelievably hard on Dianna. Witnessing her struggle to take care of me has been almost more than I can stand. However, our ultimate trust is not in one another nor is it in our ability to adjust. Our trust is in the God that put us together and has walked with us every step of the way.

In difficult days past we have relied on the promise of Scripture: "Trust in the Lord with all your heart and lean not on your own understanding. In all your ways acknowledge him and he will direct your paths" (Proverbs 3:5-6 NKJV). Those words remain the source of our confidence.

**Doubt** is another challenge that tests the faith of those battling chronic illness or disability.

I can honestly say that I have never doubted the existence of God, but I have struggled at times to trust his Word and his heart. Those moments have thankfully been brief.

We must recognize each doubt as a temptation to question God's Word or character. Our response to the temptation will determine our spiritual growth. As we persevere in faith in spite of our circumstance we become more like Christ and thus God's purposes are fulfilled in us.

If I allow myself, I can get discouraged thinking about the things I will likely never do again. Unless God does something miraculous (which he is surely capable of) or a new medication is found that not only stops the progress of the disease but also reverses past damage, the list that might be titled, "Things I Will Never Be Able to Do Again," would be long and depressing. But we all could make such a list, could we not? This is just the reality of getting older. My body simply acts older than it is.

I have said for years, MS has made me old before my time. That is true of many chronic illnesses. In time, they take a toll on the body. The same is true about the aging process in general. The longer we live on this earth the more our bodies will let us down. That makes the words of the apostle James appear even more starkly against the background of life.

Our faith is tested further, however, by the reality of just dealing with day-to-day life. Long ago, I was able to wrap my mind around the fact that God had chosen not to heal me, at least at the present time. I can live with that. It's not what I would choose. It's not the answer I want. But, it is a fact I can deal with. God is in charge and his decisions are best. It's tougher for me to deal with the everyday limitations and discomfort of my disease.

Just the day-to-day grind of being ill, dealing with limitations that keep growing in their number and severity, struggling with unrelenting symptoms can tempt you think that God really doesn't care or that his promises are untrue. In such moments I'm drawn back to God's record in my life. As Jeremiah noted as he surveyed his homeland devastated by God's judgment, "his compassions never fail. They are new every morning; great is your faithfulness" (Lamentations 3:24-25).

Ultimately, I can echo the words of Joshua, **"Now I am about to go the way of all the earth. You know with all your heart and soul that not one of all the good promises the LORD your God gave you has failed. Every promise has been fulfilled; not one has failed"** **(Joshua 23:14).**

**Discouragement** is the twin sister of doubt. Quite often, the two walk hand in hand. Where doubt raises her head, discouragement will not be far behind. Discouragement grows as we take our eyes off the goal and focus on the present circumstance. When God chose Joshua to take the place of Moses as Israel's leader in conquering the land of Canaan, he promised, "I will never leave you nor forsake you" (Joshua 1:8).

Since discouragement is the loss of courage, God challenged Joshua with these words**: "Be strong and very courageous. Because you will lead these people to inherit the land I swore to their ancestors to give them" (Joshua 1:9).** The fact that having courage is given as a command has always served as a reminder to me that courage is not something one has from birth, but rather something one chooses.

In other words, if I am discouraged or without courage in some circumstance the choice to be encouraged or courageous is mine to make. There is plenty of reason in both Scripture and in my experience with God to be courageous. I dare not allow discouragement take root in my heart. It calls into question the very character of God.

The One who promised never to leave us or forsake us commands us to trust him. We all do it imperfectly, but we cannot allow our fears or doubts or circumstances to prohibit us from trusting him or cause us to be discouraged. Paul's admonition to the Ephesians is valid for us today, "Finally, be strong in the Lord and in his mighty power "(Ephesians 6:10).

**Idleness** might seem like an odd test of faith, but I have found it to be nothing less. To some people, being disabled sounds like a great deal: no more work, no more deadlines, no more commute to work on roads clogged with commuters, no more choosing the right work clothing (every day is casual day when you don't work), and in most cases, you get a check for doing nothing (albeit a much smaller check then what you got when you worked). To the lazy person it sounds like a good deal.

The problem is that for most of us, when we lose our occupation we lose our identity. Whatever joy there is in our vastly reduced responsibilities is quickly extinguished by a lack of purpose and meaning. If most people are like me, before getting into the idea of taking disability they've spent some time, sometimes a very long time, trying to keep working in spite of the illness or infirmity.

I had known for several years that going on disability was a possibility. It was becoming increasingly difficult to manage my bladder and bowel issues on-the-job. In addition, my eyesight was worsening and the battle against fatigue was increasingly lost. Still, I wanted to work. I knew I was no longer able to pastor a church, but I was proud to be an editor of Bible study curriculum and still felt I was making a contribution to the body of Christ.

But when my health took a significant downturn in the summer of 2015, I was forced to ask myself if I could still work. It soon became evident that I could not. When I notified my employer that I would not be returning to work, I was at first relieved, but in short order I felt useless and insignificant.

As I searched the Scriptures, I was reminded that even before the Fall, God had a job for Adam to do. Adam was to tend the Garden of Eden (Genesis 2:15). I soon concluded that I needed something meaningful to do. For a time, my focus was on continuing to teach the Barnabas Project life group. I also began to think about and plan for writing a book. In time, as my eyesight worsened and my voice weakened the two tasks began to flip-flop. For some months now the focus of my time has been on writing this book.

Not every disabled person will want to be a writer, but I'm convinced we all need something meaningful and purposeful to do. When we have that, we have a reason to get up in the morning, a reason to turn the TV off, and a reason to do more than entertain ourselves.

It is not easy to force yourself to do something other than veg, but few things will be more beneficial than meaningful work. Such work does not necessarily have to include a salary, but it should include making an eternal difference. Personally, I think it is especially beneficial to leave behind a record of that which is important (a journal, book, video, audio recording) that will help your children, grandchildren, and even great-grandchildren to know what was important to you.

Satan does not hesitate to tell us no one is interested in what we have learned and that our life is without purpose or meaning, but God says just the opposite. In fact, the Israelites were commanded to pass on God's instructions from one generation to another (Deuteronomy 6).

Disability is no cause for idleness. We can talk. We can pray. We can participate in social media. Many of us can write, at least in a journal. The next generations need to hear from us. We can't let Satan use our physical limitations to sideline us in the battle.

These are but a few of the tests of faith I have encountered. Although I have not met all these challenges with joy, at least at the outset, I have found the words of James to be true. God uses these trials to make us more like Christ and thus more useful in the work of Christ if we face them with strength and courage.

# Chapter 15

## The Choice Is Yours

Let's get one thing straight. My friends and family will tell you that I'm not an over-the-top positive person nor do I advocate blind optimism. If I stub my toe or, more likely, run over it with my power chair, you won't find me praising the Lord for the ability to feel pain. You are more likely to hear, "Stupid chair!" coming out of my mouth rather than, "Praise the Lord!"

At the same time, I don't dismiss the value of a good attitude. A positive attitude can help you deal with the struggles of chronic illness, but it is not a silver bullet that solves every problem. Neither is it the sole representative of the biblical attitude toward difficulty.

As a pastor, I understand that people come to church for encouragement and they don't want to hear a "downer" of a message. (You not only catch more flies with honey than with vinegar, you also catch more parishioners.)

**FROM JONATHAN'S JOURNAL:**
*10/14/10*

*"Our Father gives only good gifts. That truth has caused me to view my MS in different light of late. Whatever the origin of my disease, it has passed through Your will before its arrival. That means You have allowed it and will use it for good in my life and in the lives of others."*

However, the Bible takes a more holistic view of life. Scripture doesn't gloss over the uncomfortable parts of life. It faces life head-on and refuses to flinch.

Even the most optimistic faith-filled individual must admit there are times in life when all is not well. On occasion, life is punctuated with grief, sorrow, and confusion. If you are in one of those times right now I want you to know it is okay to feel miserable. Sometimes, our desire to present a "victorious" example leads us to act in less than genuine ways. Outwardly, we say "Praise the Lord" and "Hallelujah" and try to act like everything's okay, but inwardly we're hanging by a thread.

Psalm 88 describes one of life's miserable situations in plain terms. The psalmist begins with the acknowledgment that God is the source of his salvation, the one to whom he cries out day and night (verses 1-2). He then immediately acknowledges that he is overwhelmed with trouble and on death's doorstep (verses 3-5).

He blames God, to an extent, considering God to be at fault for his circumstance. He says God has placed him in the lowest pit and the darkest depths. He feels God's wrath upon him, blames God for his loss of friends, and expresses feelings of being trapped (verses 6-9). Worse yet, he says he has called on the Lord every day with no answer (verses 10-14).

The psalmist laments the fact that he has suffered since his youth and repeats his charge that God's wrath has been poured out on him (verses 15-17). Finally, he concludes with despair: "You have taken from me friend and neighbor — darkness is my closest friend" (verse 18).

Unlike other psalms, Psalm 88 has no happy ending. In fact, the only positive note that is sung is in the first line, "Lord, you are the God who saves me" (verse 1). What is the cause of his negativity? Perhaps it may be found in verse 11, "From my youth I have suffered and been close to death."

Although we are given no specifics, those who battle lifelong or decades-long illness or infirmity have perhaps a greater identification with these words than the rest of the population. There are, of course, other biblical passages that are predominantly negative (the book of Lamentations comes to mind).

Chances are, you've never heard Psalm 88 read in church. It is even more unlikely that you've heard a message preached from this psalm. That's understandable, because it would make us uncomfortable. We're used to hearing a more positive message from our pulpits.

When I was a kid at youth camp, we used to sing a song that went like this:

"I'm in-right, outright, upright, downright,
Happy all the time!
I'm in-right, outright, upright, downright,
Happy all the time!
Since Jesus Christ came in and saved my soul from sin,
I'm in-right, outright, upright, downright,
Happy all the time!"

Coupled with some standup and sit-down motions, clapping hands, and a bouncy melody, this happy tune was one of my favorites. It may have expressed what we thought should be true or what we wished were true, but it was a far cry from reality in our home where my parents' divorce lurked in the shadows like a big cat waiting to pounce. But, it wasn't just our home. The Christian life is simply not *happy all the time* and the Bible reflects that.

I say this simply to ease the pain and frustration of those whose life does not measure up to this "happy all the time" standard. Life hurts sometimes and there's no use denying it. If you live long enough you are sure to have some Psalm 88 days. I'm not suggesting that every day should be like Psalm 88, but I am suggesting that there may be times when this psalm best expresses the feelings of the person battling chronic illness and there is no shame in that.

If darkness feels like your closest friend these days don't beat yourself up over it. It is not wrong to feel that way. It is not even wrong to express that feeling to God. Remember, Jesus prayed on the cross, "My God, my God, why have you forsaken me?" (Matthew 27:20). It is okay if you don't feel victorious today. There are better days ahead.

One of the more frustrating aspects of my multiple sclerosis has been the way it has taken many activities off the table for me. Many people envision their retirement as the time to travel, but traveling is difficult for me. Some people are spending retirement at the beach.

Others are spending it on the lake. For the most part, those options have been removed by my illness.

However, although there are many things in life we don't get to choose, one thing we do have a choice about is how we approach each day. I'm not talking about mouthing sappy sweet sayings we often find on cute posters or desktops. I'm referring to making a conscious decision to focus on what is right instead of wrong in our world.

With that in mind, I took a few minutes and sat down one day when I was feeling low and wrote the following list:

Reasons to be Encouraged Today
1. Jesus loves me.
2. My sins are forgiven.
3. I'm not who I was.
4. My wife loves me beyond reason.
5. My children love me.
6. I have many great friends.
7. I still have a ministry.
8. I'm not destitute.
9. I have plenty to eat today.
10. I have a comfortable home.
11. I have a comfortable recliner.
12. Randall House (my former employer) has been good to me.
13. God is in control.
14. God's resources are limitless.
15. I'm not confined to bed.
16. I'm not in the hospital.
17. I don't have to eat puréed food. (Been there, done that, no *likey*,)
18. Grace.

19. Sovereignty.
20. I still get to teach (at church).
21. God is always faithful.
22. God's intentions are good.
23. My children follow Christ.
24. My parents follow Christ.
25. My wife follows Christ.
26. My in-laws follow Christ.
27. My hope in Christ is secure.
28. I have caregivers to help me.
29. I have a computer.
30. Jesus paid it all.
31. Prayer changes things.
32. For those who love him, God works all things for good.
33. God can do way more than I ask.
34. With God, nothing is impossible.
35. God is using even MS for my good.
36. I had no injuries from my most recent fall.
37. I'm enjoying another day of life.

Looking at this list today I could think of many more items to add, but these are the ones I came up with on that particular day. I made the list because I was struggling with discouragement and writing the list changed my day. Nothing else changed but my attitude. The next time you are struggling with discouragement I would suggest the same prescription for you.

I have found it most helpful to occasionally list the reasons to be encouraged. This is beneficial because it gets my focus off what is discouraging and puts it on the positive. It helps to write the list in some form because it gives me something to go back to on down days. I don't always have to write a new list because the same reasons are still valid.

I'm no psychologist, but sometime back I realized I had been doing self-talk for years. When I was a kid, and feeling pressure or anxiety, I would say to myself, "I'll be glad when Christmas gets here." Then, I would think about all the fun I had previously at Christmas time and I would anticipate and try to imagine the fun I'd have next Christmas.

When summer youth camp was a key part of my life, I would say, "I'll be glad when it time for camp." When I started playing Little League baseball I would say, "I'll be glad when our next game gets here!" And I would try to imagine how much fun it would be.

When my parents divorced, I would spend the school year with my dad in California and then fly to Oklahoma to spend at least portions of summer with my mom. I enjoyed traveling alone because it made me feel grown-up. So that began a new stage of self-talk in which I said, "I'll be glad when school is out."

**FROM JONATHAN'S JOURNAL:**
*10/30/98*

*"How many more years do I have on this earth? Only You know, but the number doesn't matter. For one day I will indeed leave this life behind, but my life will not end. Eternity in Your presence awaits. Though I die, yet shall I live. What to do with what time I have here? I will love and enjoy You, love others, love my wife, kids, and other family, and seek to share the good news of abundant eternal Christ with as many as You allow."*

I continued this pattern after I graduated high school with things like, "I'll be glad when it's basketball season," or "I'll be glad when it's Christmas break." Eventually, it became "I'll be glad when Dianna and I are married." Then, I just naturally continued my "I'll be glad when" pattern with whatever I was looking forward to.

When MS entered the picture my self-talk changed. Rather than looking forward to something good, I began to focus on what I was feeling here and now. I began to catch myself saying, "I don't feel very good today" and "I'll be glad when I feel better." The problem was I didn't feel very good every day and the chances that I would feel better were not good. I merely reinforced how badly I felt, and the fact that it was unlikely to change, over and over again.

The natural result of this negative reinforcement was depression. When I finally realized what I was doing to myself I had to change my focus. I had to learn to focus on what was right with my world rather than what was wrong. I had to quit allowing my physical feelings to influence my mood. In addition, I decided I had to quit putting off "being glad" until some future date and determine I would be glad today, right now, matter what was wrong.

I began to be thankful for the little things and stop rehearsing things that were wrong. For instance, I learned to find joy in having a little energy, owning an assistive device to help me get around (cane, walker, scooter, power chair, etc.), having people to assist me, or even having a regular bowel movement. (Sorry, that last one was a little too much information, wasn't it?) As my focus changed, so did my mood and, to an extent, my physical feelings improved.

The human body is sometimes like an insistent puppy that crawls all over you, licks your face, and nudges your hand until you pet it. It seems like no matter which way you turn it is right there in your face. Unfortunately, it is not nearly so cute and cuddly, either.

Like everyone else, chronically ill or disabled people have a choice about how to approach each day. I discovered that if I thought much about it I could find reasons to feel bad, but if I intentionally looked for reasons to be thankful and to find joy I would feel much better.

For me, this included not rehearsing my symptoms with everyone who asked, "How are you today?" If I responded to that question with an inventory of my symptoms (my legs are tired, I'm battling muscle spasms, my hands feel like I have gloves on, my feet feel like they are crossed though they are not, I am exhausted, I have double vision, etc.) I would feel no better and I would have less friends.

Thus, my most common response to the question, "How are you?" is "I am fine, how are you?" There are, of course, some people with whom I will share more of how I feel, but they are few indeed. What I enjoy most is sharing with others the blessings God has brought into my life.

There was a time in my life when I thought it was dishonest to say I was doing fine when I was not. I came to realize, however, that most people don't really want a rundown of your symptoms, they simply want to express that they care. Telling them "I am fine" conveys what they need to know: I still have MS and I have had no major change in my symptoms.

I would like to suggest, however, that others learn a new way of greeting or making small talk besides asking how you're feeling. A better approach might be, "It's so good to see you! I hope you're having a good day." That approach shows concern but doesn't make physical feelings the focus.

When it comes to choosing your attitude, Barbara Toye was perhaps the best I've ever known. She was one of my favorite people. Barbara and her husband Les, a retired schoolteacher, attended our church in Garden Grove for several years. Barbara was blind, the result of severe diabetes. She had numerous other health issues as well and Christian radio was a lifeline for her.

Our church advertised on a local Christian talk station for about six months. During that time, they invited me to be a guest on several of their programs. Barbara heard me on that station and when she found I was in the same area as her, she came to meet me. Barbara and Les were the only two people that actually came to our church and stayed there as a result of the advertising, but they made it all worthwhile.

In spite of her physical struggles, Barbara was energetic and positive. She never ceased to amaze me with her zest for following Christ. One of my most memorable moments with Barbara occurred when I was having lunch with her and several of our senior Saints. I had to excuse myself early because I had a funeral to conduct. After I said goodbye, just before I turned to leave, Barbara said, "Preach Jesus to them, Jonathan!" I assured her I would do so.

Barbara's heart was to see people come to Christ. She was eager to pray and more than willing to help with anything she could. This woman with everything to be discouraged about found reasons for encouragement, not just for herself but for others as well. Rather than moan over what she could not do, Barbara looked for what she could do to minister to others.

Les was an exemplary husband. His love for Barbara was obvious through his actions in unselfishly caring for her. In spite of his heavy load, Les maintained a patient and sweet spirit and a level head, focusing on what Barbara could do instead of what she could not.

One night, Barbara went to bed like usual. At some point in the night the Lord took her home to be with him. I had the privilege of conducting her funeral and yes, I "preached Jesus" to them, but I was playing second fiddle. Barbara had been preaching Jesus to them for years by the way she conducted her life.

Now it's our turn.

# Chapter 16

## Prognosis

Where do we go from here? What does the future hold? How long will I live? Will I still be alive when Christ returns? Will I live into my 60s? 70s? 80s? 90s?

I don't have answers to those questions. None of us do. If my nearly 6 decades of life have taught me anything it is that life on this planet is precarious.

Janet, my third-grade classmate, was sitting at her desk next to mine before Christmas break 1966. She was all smiles and giggles, looking forward to Christmas. When we came back to school in January, her desk was empty. Janet, her sister,

FROM JONATHAN'S JOURNAL: *1/25/11 "Eternal Judge, I glory in Your promise of a house not made with hands, eternal in the heavens (2 Corinthians 5:1). Father, I am so focused on this flesh that I sometimes fail to live with the eternity in view. I easily become focused on how I feel, what my work schedule is like, and my needs that I failed to remain even aware that this body, this life, this work, and this stuff, is all temporary. What matters most is not what I get done, how I am perceived, or what I achieve. All that matters is that I please You."*

and their parents were all killed in a tragic car accident. They were the victims of a drunk driver.

A kid I played baseball with died when I was in fifth grade. Crossing the street on his bicycle, near a railroad crossing, he was hit by car. The driver never saw him until it was too late.

When I was in sixth grade, I believe, a nursing home resident was on my paper route. I took her paper to her room every day. One day when I arrived the woman at the front desk stopped me and said that patient would not be taking the paper anymore. I was immediately distressed, thinking I'd somehow offended her. The lady assured me that it was not my fault; the patient had merely passed away.

Since those early introductions to the reality of death, I have learned that death is no respecter of persons. I have conducted funerals for infants whose lifespan was but a whisper. I have witnessed others hold death at bay for 100 years or more. Eventually, death snatched even them.

The longer you live on this earth, the more friends you will lose to death's icy grip. Much of what we do for entertainment or leisure does little more than to distract us from the temporary nature and seeming futility of life.

People sometimes wonder if multiple sclerosis is terminal. The answer is no, usually it is not. It's actually rare to see an obituary that lists MS as a cause of death. The most common language seems to be, he or she "died from complications of multiple sclerosis." Even that language is becoming rarer as the disease modifying therapies get better.

But the reality is, regardless of the cause, most of us will die. Of course, those who are alive when Christ returns will avoid death but will be changed "in the twinkling of an eye"(1 Corinthians 15:55).

The truth is, if you have a hangnail, you're terminal. The cause of death remains to be determined, but the inevitability of death is indisputable.

So what is my long-term prognosis? I'm going to die. So are you. Unless we are among the privileged few who are alive when Christ returns (and our odds are getting better as his return grows nearer; but that's a book I'll let someone else write), we're going to enter eternity through the doorway of death.

How am I going to die? That is anybody's guess. Who knows? I may die in a skydiving accident. (I know it would be an accident because I'm not about to jump out of a plane on purpose.) I might even die as a result of being shot out of a cannon at a circus, but that does not seem likely, either.

God certainly knows if, when, how, and why I will die, but Jesus said, "I am the resurrection and the life. The one who believes in me will live, even though they die; and whoever lives by believing in me will never die. Do you believe this?" (John 11:25-26).

I will die. I will exit this world. I may do it in a flame of glory (not likely), or I may do it with one final gasp in a hospital somewhere, but on the basis of the promise of Jesus Christ, though I die physically I will live forever.

Many years ago, I received a phone call from a nearby hospital late one night after I had gone to bed. A patient there in ICU wanted to see me. Leonard was a member of the first church I pastored. I had the privilege of helping him come to faith in Christ and learn how to follow Jesus. However, I had recently resigned as the pastor of that church. Still, Leonard wanted to see me.

When I arrived in the ICU, Leonard was anxious. He thanked me for coming and said he just needed to talk to me. "I'm going to die tonight," he said, as though it was well known. Then, in his usual polite manner, he asked, "Would you just read to me some of those passages about heaven?" I, of course, agreed to do so.

I believe I read several passages of Scripture that night, but when I got to these verses Leonard seem to drink them in like a thirsty man guzzles water:

"Do not let your hearts be troubled. You believe in God; believe also in me. My Father's house has many rooms; if that were not so, would I have told you that I'm going there to prepare a place for you? And if I go and prepare a place for you, I will come back and take you to be with me that you may be where I am" (John 14:1-3).

"That's it!" Leonard interrupted. "That's what I wanted to hear. Is that true?"

"Yes, that's true. The Bible says a lot about heaven," I replied.

"I just needed to hear it," he explained. "I'm going to die tonight, and I just want to be ready." Leonard seemed much calmer now and more at peace. I concluded my visit with prayer, thanking God for the promise of heaven. I tried to assure Leonard that I would see him the next day, but he seemed unconvinced.

"Well, if I don't see you tomorrow," I concluded with a smile, "I'll look you up when I get to heaven." Leonard managed to smile back.

I stopped at the nurses' station on my way out of ICU and asked about Leonard. "How is he doing? Is he in any danger of dying?"

"Oh, no, not at all," she assured me. "He's doing fine. He is actually scheduled to move to a regular room tomorrow."

I left the hospital, chalking up Leonard's words to anxiety or medication, and drove home. I hadn't been at the house very long until the phone rang. It was the hospital. Leonard was dead.

Did Leonard have a premonition about his death? Did he get a word from the Lord about what was to happen? Was it merely a self-fulfilling prophecy? Did Leonard become convinced he was going to die and somehow willed it to happen? I don't know the answers. Leonard never told me why he thought he was going to die that night and I never thought to ask him.

If Leonard did have advance notice that he was going to die that night then he was an unusual man. Most people, with the possible exception of prisoners facing execution, don't get that kind of notice. But logic and observation tell us that the day will come for us like it has for everyone else that has gone before us.

If we have any delusions about death, God has put us on notice. Hebrews 9:27 says, ". . . people are destined to die once, and after that to face judgment . . ." Death is one appointment we all keep, and we won't be late.

For the believer, the Christ-follower, death is only a doorway into something far greater — eternity with Christ! We don't know all the details about heaven, but if we believe the Bible we know it to be a very real place. Heaven is the place of no more sorrow, no more pain, no more disability, and no more disappointments. It is the place of no more goodbyes but an eternal hello.

As I write this today I think of so many that in human estimation were taken from this earth too soon. I think of many more drawing closer day by day saying the inevitable goodbye to friends and family. I think of some for whom goodbye is likely to come before they want it — before they get married, before their kids get married, before the grandchildren come along, or before they accomplish the goals on their bucket list.

I think of still others for whom their day of departure is long overdue, at least in their minds. They have had enough of life in this broken world. They are weary of loneliness, or pain, or disability, or grief, or poverty, or injustice, or addiction, etc. These folks are just weary. Many of them suffer with chronic illness. Believe me, some days I can relate.

As I've said previously, I feel the emotion Asaph expressed in Psalm 88:18, "You have taken from me friend and neighbor — darkness is my closest friend." Some days it feels like that, but I refuse to stay there. Instead, I'd rather take my cues from another psalm of Asaph, Psalm 73.

After confessing his envy of the wicked who seemed to prosper while he suffered, the psalmist came to some powerful conclusions:

"Yet I am always with you; you hold me by my right hand. You guide me with your counsel, and afterward you will take me into glory.
Whom have I in heaven but you?
And earth has nothing I desire besides you.
My flesh and my heart may fail, but God is the strength of my heart and my portion forever"
(Psalm 73:23-26).

The future for Asaph is the same as the future for Jonathan and it is the same as a future for all who follow Christ:

1. God will always hold our hands, no matter what the future holds.
2. God will guide us with his counsel, no matter where the road takes us.
3. God will take us into glory.
4. Nothing on this earth is comparable to God.
5. Though flesh and heart fail, God will be our strength and portion forever.

If you are a follower of Jesus Christ, you can count on these things. Your health may change. Your friends may abandon you. Your family may let you down. Your circumstances, perish the thought, may get worse. But God will be with you no matter what.

As a kid, I often based my courage on whether Dad would be with me. I wasn't a particularly courageous child, but the presence of my dad was enough to assure me that I would be fine, no matter what the circumstance.

Unfortunately, I discovered one day my dad wasn't superhuman. We were picking peaches one summer to supplement our income. As I recall, Dad was coming down the ladder when he stepped on a rotten peach and slipped. He fell to the ground, landing on his back. The fully loaded metal peach bucket hanging around his neck flew up and hit him on the head, opening a gash just above his eyebrow.

At that moment, lying on the ground, clearly dazed and bleeding, Dad didn't look like such a superhero. I realized for the first time my dad was just a man as subject to the law of gravity as I was, and just as likely to be hurt by it.

The disciples, however, saw in Jesus a man who could circumvent the laws of nature by walking on water, turning water into wine, and even raising the dead. When they did eventually see Jesus broken, bloodied, and crucified they were forced to face the fact he was a man. But three days later he rose from the dead to prove he was also God.

It is this God that promises to be with us whatever the future may bring, to guide us every step of the way, and to take us to a glorious home that far excels anything this earth has to offer.

What does the immediate future hold for me? Will I gain strength? Will I walk again? Will I ever be able to care for myself again? Will I end up in a nursing home? Will I just continue like I am until something else arises to complicate matters and eventually take my life?

Again, I can't answer those questions today. None of us can. We can, however, rest in the words of the apostle Paul: "I consider that our present sufferings are not worth comparing with the glory that will be revealed in us" (Romans 8:18).

If you have a chronic illness or disability I have good news for you: The end is in sight and it is glorious! Our present sufferings, and any that come our way in the future, can never eclipse the joy and glory awaits us in eternity with Christ!

Yes, this life can be dark. Perhaps especially so when chronic illness or disability is involved, yet, there is hope in Jesus Christ. Our suffering is temporal; it won't last forever. But the hope in Christ is eternal. By the grace of God, and to his glory alone, it is in Christ, that I find I hope, even in the darkness.

"For our light and momentary troubles are achieving for us an eternal glory that far outweighs them all" (2 Corinthians 4:17).

# *Soli Deo Gloria*

Made in the USA
San Bernardino, CA
07 January 2018